# Seeing Yourself
as a Teacher

# Seeing Yourself as a Teacher

## Conversations with Five New Teachers in a University Writing Program

Elizabeth Rankin
University of North Dakota

National Council of Teachers of English
1111 W. Kenyon Road, Urbana, Illinois 61801-1096

Manuscript Editor: Mimi L. Mukerjee/Humanities & Sciences Associates

Production Editor: Michael G. Ryan

Interior Design: Tom Kovacs for TGK Design

Cover Design: Loren Kirkwood

NCTE Stock Number: 42982–3050

It is the policy of NCTE in its journals and other publications to provide a forum for the open discussion of ideas concerning the content and the teaching of English and the language arts. Publicity accorded to any particular point of view does not imply endorsement by the Executive Committee, the Board of Directors, or the membership at large, except in announcements of policy, where such endorsement is clearly specified.

**Library of Congress Cataloging-in-Publication Data**

Rankin, Elizabeth Deane.
    Seeing yourself as a teacher : conversations with five new
teachers in a university writing program / Libby Rankin.
      p.    cm.
    Includes bibliographical references and index.
    ISBN 0-8141-4298-2
    1. English language—Rhetoric—Study and teaching—United States.
2. Creative writing (Higher education)—United States.  3. English
teachers—United States—Interviews.  4. College teachers—United
States—Interviews.  I. Title.
PE1405.U6R36  1994
808'.042'071173—dc20
                              94-15673
                              CIP

# Contents

# Note

All of the names in this book except mine have been changed to protect the privacy of the research participants.

Most of the quoted passages in this manuscript are drawn from transcripts of recorded interviews with the five graduate students in my study. Although I have not tried to capture every nuance of these conversations—every pause, false start, interruption—I have tried to maintain the flavor of the spoken voices. In some cases, passages have been edited to delete irrelevant or repetitious material; such places are marked by ellipses. Except for isolated instances where a word is italicized for emphasis, italics indicate passages excerpted from written texts.

# Preface

## Spring

I am teaching the "Seminar on Teaching College English" to a class of twelve first-year graduate teaching assistants. This year, I have determined to do it differently, to put more emphasis on the writing they do, to let them take control of the class. Nevertheless, I have chosen readings, and I have asked the class to respond to them, in writing, in class discussions, and once while I am out of town, in small groups. At first I am surprised by their reactions. They resist almost everything—even each other. While I am out of town, they become a dysfunctional family, competing for authority in the small groups, going silent, refusing the tasks I have left for them. When I come back, I am disappointed and angry—but I am also tired. It is sixteen years now that I have been teaching, half that time as a temporary instructor, half as a regular faculty member. The year has been an exhausting one for me, fighting battles with my colleagues over hiring, interviewing for jobs elsewhere, myself. I have a year of leave coming up, and I don't feel like fighting this TA seminar. Somewhere I stumble across Jane Tompkins's "Pedagogy of the Distressed" (1990), and it gives me permission to let go. I let go.

It's funny what happens when a person like me lets go. For one thing, not everyone notices. Months later, I find myself talking with one of these TAs about letting go, and she laughs at my concern: "People like us," she says, "don't have to worry about being irresponsible. People like us couldn't be irresponsible if we tried." Maybe she's right. But at the time, I can't see it. Tompkins or no Tompkins, I feel like I'm not doing my job.

At midterm, the TAs turn in drafts of their teaching narratives—essays designed to evoke and reflect on some aspect of their fall teaching experience. Mike Rose's *Lives on the Boundary* (1989) has been a model of sorts, here—but given their reaction to Rose (one person excoriated his writing style), I don't know what to expect. I take the drafts with me to Minneapolis over spring break and begin reading them in the car on the way home. At first, I am simply relieved: the assignment has "worked" as I hoped it would. The stories they tell are rich with remembered experiences—the gut-wrenching fear when you meet that first class, the betrayal of trust when a student plagiarizes, the frustration at a student who rejects your best efforts to reach him, the anger at a peer who openly criticizes your work. And in nearly all of these drafts is an element of reflection, a sense that the writer has grown beyond the narrated experience, that the process of writing itself has assisted that growth.

Then, I realize that something else is going on here. Two of the narratives are more than good—they are stunning! In one piece, a young woman TA takes her class outside to watch freight trains from the overpass. Interwoven through her essay—a complex personal meditation on freedom, authority, and resistance—are fragments of her students' writing, writing so powerful that I can hardly believe it comes from eighteen-year-olds. Another narrative takes off in a Joycean mode—a portrait of the teacher as a young man in love with language—but turns Kafkaesque when the young TA is called in by the campus police. Apparently, a chance remark he made in class has frightened one of his students, a young woman recently raped by an unknown attacker. The narrative ends with the TA's frustrated attempts to tell the story to his father, whose well-meaning but nervous response sounds familiar. I recognize it as my own response when he reported the incident to me, his teaching supervisor, last semester.

Intrigued by what I have seen in the narrative essays, I find myself looking past unfocused seminar discussions to the other writing these TAs are doing. I have mixed responses to the reading journals: It's clear that some people just aren't doing the reading. Or they're reading only enough to spark a response for the journal. Still, I have to admit that I share some of their impatience with the academic tenor of some of our readings. What they have to say of their own teaching experience is often just as pertinent, and it speaks to me with an immediacy that I don't find in the academic work.

By the time we reach the end of the semester, and I am reading their informal case studies, I realize something important is going on here. In fact, I am tempted to say that this rowdy, resistant group of TAs is learning more, from reading their own teaching, than my more dutiful groups in the past had learned from reading the experts. But I can't say for sure. What I can say is that I am learning. I am learning to listen. I am learning to think about teaching. I am learning, finally, that what I have to offer these new teachers is balanced equally by what they have to offer me.

In July, I begin my year's sabbatical. I am suddenly free to pursue my own research interests. But by now, I know that I won't be going far. I have determined to spend my leave as I spent last semester: listening to new teachers struggle with what it means to teach writing, and reflecting on what I can learn—what we all can learn—in the process.

# Introduction

## Fall

It is the second week of classes and already Meredith has a story to tell. It's one of those VCR horror stories: you've arranged to show a video in your composition class, but you can't get the machine to work. "I know this story," I tell her. And I do. We all do. First the TV won't come on, then the VCR won't come on and the cassette won't go in. Meanwhile, time's wasting and you're getting more and more flustered. As you squat by the machine cart with your back to the students, you hear them whispering and mumbling and calling out instructions, and you imagine the smirks they're trading at your expense. Finally, ten minutes into the class, you get the thing going and retire to the back of the room, where you can hide while they watch the movie. I know the next part of the story, too. As Meredith tells it, I can almost feel it in my gut:

> And I felt this old, really nasty feeling that I used to get when I first started teaching. I mean, I don't know how to describe it, it's this really—I guess it's fear, but it's also, it's fear of making a fool out of yourself and this sense that they're the enemy and that they've turned on you somehow. And so I told myself, "If you don't make this feeling go away when you get up, you're gonna lose—" It really scared me . . . 'cause when that used to happen I would get, like angry at the class, I mean I would, because I was so tensed up I would be very detached and—know what I'm talking about? So I said, "Well, this is what I've been afraid of actually," 'cause everything's been going good in the meantime and maybe that was what I was afraid of. You know, what if that old feeling comes back?

Ah yes, that old feeling. I know it well, even after sixteen years of teaching. As I listen to Meredith narrate her experience, I'm reminded of certain anxiety dreams I still have: Me, bumbling and incompetent at the blackboard, frantically trying to remember what class I'm teaching. Behind me, the snickers, the giggles, the slamming of books and scraping of chairs. Tense and nervous, I turn to face the students, but they're already out of their seats, out the door. I call out, tell them to take their seats, but they're already gone. They know I have no control here.

But wait—whose story is this? Is it Meredith's story, or mine? As I listen, already the boundaries are blurred. On the one hand, it *is* her story—and she tells it well. It has a beginning, which I've summarized above, a middle, where I've left you hanging, and an end, which I'll return to in a moment. It also has a theme, and because Meredith is the person she is, that theme has great personal significance.

On the other hand, it's my story, too, as Meredith suggests when she offers it to me: "I have a story for you," she says. Does she know that I will recognize this story, that it echoes my own experience as a teacher? Or does she simply think of it as a gift, something I can use in the book I will write from these interviews? And what do I mean when I tell her "I know this story"? Do I know it only because I see myself in Meredith, or because I have seen so many new teachers go through this experience? For me, the VCR story serves as a perfect beginning, for it captures a sense of where so many new teachers begin: with the fears and the doubts, with the first painful efforts to see themselves as teachers, to believe what the university implied when it hired them as graduate teaching assistants: that they are qualified, and competent, and resourceful, and smart, and that they know what they're doing in the classroom.

For some teaching assistants, this role is not so hard to imagine. They are already experienced high school teachers. Or they come, at least, with student-teaching or peer-tutoring experience, and that experience, however thin it might be, gives them confidence to believe that in fact they *can* teach college writing. Many TAs, however, have no such resources to draw on. They arrive on our campuses fresh out of undergraduate programs in literature or creative writing (or psychology, biology, education, or French), attend a one- or two-week fall workshop, and the next week assume sole responsibility for one or two sections of the university's required first-year writing course. Is it any wonder they fear the judgment of students who may see right through them? What's amazing, when I think about it, is how many survive it: how quickly they learn and how capably they manage.

Take Meredith, for instance. Her story doesn't end where I interrupted it. As she sits in the back of the darkened room, watching the last half of the movie with her students, she uses this respite to collect herself and plan what to do next. One thing she must do, she realizes, is to put herself in charge again. With the final credits rolling across the screen, and the movie's theme music playing in the background, she gets up and begins to hand back papers, reestablishing, in an almost physical sense, a feeling of authority and control.

Interestingly, though, this is not the crucial moment for Meredith—the crucial moment comes after she's given back the papers, when she returns to the front of the class to lead the discussion. She's chosen this movie, *The Breakfast Club*, because it's about teenagers struggling to find out who they are and because she thinks her students will see themselves in its characters. Now that they've seen the movie, she will ask them to write about similar experiences in their own lives, but first she asks if they identify with any of the characters they've just seen. Here's how she tells it:

> And so I let a couple of people talk, and then I was sitting on the desk, on top of the desk instead of behind it, and I said, "Well, I'll tell you what I was thinking when I was at the back of the room." I said, "I was thinking that I really ... identify with Brian" [a character who makes a lamp in his shop class but then can't get it to work]. So I said, "I know exactly what he feels like, because that's the same way I felt when I couldn't get this VCR started" [laughs]. And they started, you know, I could just feel the whole room loosen then, and so then that just set me off, and I went on talking about how that was something that I had trouble with, 'cause I couldn't tell direction, and I couldn't do the spatial relations things on aptitude tests, you know? ... And I said, if we had to show a movie again ... the same thing would happen to me again. I really got going then. [laughs] ... I said that if we did it again I still couldn't plug the thing in because for some reason it doesn't register in my brain—which is the truth, it doesn't, and it really does, it frustrates me.... But, it was like they—I don't know—I mean it just diffused the whole thing. And I mean, I got everything back. . . . When I felt that kind of feeling I thought, "Well, I'm zooming backwards, ... all the ground that I've covered is totally gone." But it just came back ... It reminded me of what hell it was in the beginning, 'cause I was like that all the time.

As I listen to Meredith tell her story, I feel happy with her. She got it all back—all that ground she had covered. And not accidentally, either: "If you don't make this feeling go away," she had told herself when it started, "you're gonna lose [all that ground]." So she made it go away. She used strategies she had learned through experience, first to claim (or reclaim) her authority, then to release it. And now here she is telling me the story, even laughing at herself a little bit, and going on about her business.

In the pages that follow, I'll have more to say about Meredith, and I'll introduce you to four of her colleagues, as well. All five are young graduate students in their third semester of teaching writing at a medium-size state university. Except for Meredith, who taught briefly as a TA in another discipline, they had no teaching experience when they began the graduate program last year. All were students in a seminar on "Teaching College English" the previous spring, where they wrote the narratives and informal case studies that inspired this research project. And all agreed, shortly afterward, to take part in the project, meeting with me weekly through the fall semester to talk about their teaching, then reading through the transcripts of our con-versations and meeting again in the spring to reflect on the meaning of their experience.

Listening to the voices of these TAs, reading their words, you may remember, as I did, what it's like to begin teaching: to negotiate the complex and often conflicting roles of student and teacher, to develop some strategies that feel comfortable, some theories that make sense. Above all, you may remember how scary the whole experience was, and how exhilarating. And perhaps you'll remember how important it is from time to time to step back and see yourself as a teacher.

# 1 Taking It Personally

In the beginning, I ask them all the same question: "When you think about last year, if you close your eyes and look back on the whole year of teaching, what images come to mind? What do you see?"

Alex pauses, closes his eyes. "Hmmm . . . A lot of faces. I see all the faces of the students." When I press him for specifics, Alex recalls one particular student, Glenn:

> A guy that sat against the wall, closest to the door. He was always the first one out. And he was just one of those that Harley [another TA] says is aggressively apathetic. He didn't care, you know. I mean, the first time, I sat down and talked to him outside, I said, "How come you don't talk in class? Don't you like to talk?" "I don't mind talkin'." "You don't talk in class and when I call on you, one word responses." "Yeah." You know, that's about as far as it went, and he didn't—he was one of those that you notice is not putting effort into it and doesn't care to put effort into it, doesn't want to be in this room, perhaps doesn't even want to be in college, and that was a real weird experience, when I realized that: This person does not want to be here. This person would rather be off in the park partying with his friends, and you wonder, why are you, why is this person here?

Of all the students Alex taught last year, this is the one he remembers most vividly. Why, I wonder, does Glenn stick in his mind?

Later in the semester, I get a clue. It's the fifth week of classes and Alex mentions something a student has said in class:

> It was interesting today as one of the girls said, "Well I finally figured out that I actually have to work here, while I'm in school, I actually have to work." I said, "You're ahead of the game; it took me a year and a half to figure that out" [laughs]. And it did, I was just kinda drifting; I was just *there* for a year and a half—which I think was a good experience because then I figured out why, and what I wanted—[laughs].

When I ask if his experience gives him an advantage with his students, enables him to empathize with them, Alex says he thinks that's possible. His memories, he says, are still fresh enough that he can relate to what the students are going through:

> I can remember the exact day, I was sitting down in the [campus pub], I was having a beer, I'm like, "Well, what the hell am I doing here?" I was looking at my architecture book that I was supposed to be reading and wasn't, and thinking, "What do I want to do? What am I here for? I don't really want to be an architect. What do I want to do? . . . " And then I decided, "Well, if I'm here to be in school to learn something, I'd better do that instead of all the partying, all the going out and that stuff." That was—I can still remember that.

As he thinks about his own experience, Alex goes on to philosophize about his students:

> But I think everybody has to come to that conclusion on their own. You can't sit 'em down and say in class, "Now you better figure out that this class, composition, is gonna matter. . . . " So I just try to help along the ones who have figured [out] what they want, right now. I think that's what we have to concentrate on, those few students maybe that have figured out that, "Yes, I want to be here; yes, I want to learn." Not to ignore the other ones but to recognize that if they don't take to writing, then OK, they're not taking to their physics class, their chemistry class, and their business class, either.

Something in what Alex says here reminds me of our earlier conversation. Is this why he remembers Glenn, I wonder? Is Glenn some manifestation of his former self? Then I recall an incident from my own teaching career. It was ten years ago, at another university, and I was having trouble with a student in one of my classes. As I told a colleague about the situation, I found I couldn't explain it very well. Somehow, an ugly tension had grown up between this student and me, and it was spreading to the rest of the class. "Do you see any of yourself in this student?" my colleague asked. I must have hesitated. "I ask because I've noticed that in myself," she went on. "The students who give me the most trouble are often the students who are like me in some way." Yes, I thought. That makes sense. This student *does* remind me of myself as a student. She has all my worst traits!

In my case, the identification of student and teacher was a source of tension. For Alex, though, at least on the surface, it's different. For him, seeing himself in his students is a way of empathizing—but at the same time distancing himself from his students. Because he has shared their backgrounds, their uncertainty about who they are and where they're headed, he doesn't take it personally when the students cut class, fall asleep, do less than stellar work. Or at least he doesn't seem to. One could argue, I suppose, that the mere fact that Alex remembers Glenn, out of all the students he had last year, is evidence that he hasn't "chalked it up" as easily as he says he has. If he had truly not been bothered by Glenn's "aggressively apathetic" attitude, if he had truly been concentrating on those students who had figured out why they were in school, wouldn't he have remembered their faces more vividly than Glenn's?

Reviewing the tapes of our conversations now, I find myself speculating about answers to this question—and to similar questions that come up in other interviews, as well as in my reflections on my own teaching. Why do we remember particular faces? Why do certain students manage to get our goat? What accounts for the intense interest we develop in some of our students? Why do some teachers get more involved with their students than others? Sometimes, the TAs themselves speculate about such questions, calling my attention to patterns in the finely threaded webs that connect them to their students. Sometimes though, it is I, not they, who see patterns, sense connections, just the way my former colleague, hearing me complain about that troublesome student, sensed a connection between the student and me.

When I find myself in this situation, speculating about other people's meanings, writing about other people's lives, I feel uncomfortable about my researcher role. Who am I to say what is going on in these teacher/student relationships? Who am I to read into those relationships complex, unacknowledged emotions and motives? One answer, I suppose, lies in the language I've just used. I am a reader. And like any reader—of fiction, of the world—I bring to my reading my own set of complex, sometimes unacknowledged, intentions and expectations. As reader, I am more than just researcher. I am teacher, woman, daughter, sister, lover, friend, colleague—all my various selves. What I see in the TAs is always, inevitably, some reflection of my own experience. So I plunge ahead, reading the TAs, reading their students, reading (always) myself.

## Defining Terms

In common parlance, when we "take teaching personally," it may mean something positive—that we have integrated who we are as teachers with who we are as human beings. Or it may mean something more negative—that we haven't learned to draw boundaries between the various roles we play. Of course the notion that there even *are* such boundaries—that we can or should separate the professional and personal domains—is in itself highly problematic. But most of us would probably agree that the student/teacher relationship depends to some extent upon our being able to negotiate some kind of balance between the personal and the professional in our own lives, and upon our ability to recognize and respect the boundaries our students construct between their academic and personal lives. In this chapter, I can't begin to account for all the ways new teachers "take teaching personally," but I will consider how the personal infuses these TAs' dealings with their students, and thus how it influences what and how they teach.

### Peer or Professor?

Negotiating a balance between the personal and the professional in our lives is always difficult, but it can be especially tricky for new teachers who are not yet used to their teacher roles, and who often are close to their students in age and in personal background. For graduate teaching assistants, the situation is intensified by the fact that they *are* still students, and thus share with their own students a similar status and common experiences.

As it happens, all five TAs in my study are in their twenties. Though many TAs in our program are older and have teaching experience of one kind or another, in this group only Meredith has taught before, and only briefly, as a graduate student in another discipline. What this means is that all five TAs are very much new to their roles as writing teachers and still uncertain about how to define their relationships with their students. In one conversation, Peter recalls a moment in his first year of teaching which captures the complexity of the TA's position:

> [I'm] sitting in a room with an English Department meeting going on, you know, with these professionals. And . . . it's like I'm right on the door, you know. In the hallway are the kids, the students running past, and the other part is me trying to listen to this meeting, you know, and I'm doing both things at once . . . and I can't help but think that that has to be pretty hard.

Peter's language reveals the dilemma he finds himself in. At 28, a new TA, he is neither "kid" nor "professional," neither fish nor fowl, and he's bewildered about how to behave in this strange world of graduate school.

For Mike, 27, the issue is how his students perceive him. This semester, he's particularly aware of their perceptions because he has volunteered to teach a 200-level "Business and Technical Writing" class, and his students tend to be older:

I get this impression that they're real conscious of the fact that I'm—I sort of feel that they think I'm too young to be teaching this course or probably too young to really know what I'm doing as a teacher, which in a sense is true, but—which *is* true. Not too young to do it, I can do it, but there are some weak spots and I do run into problems, and so they perceive, I feel that they perceive this as a weakness.

Later in the semester he's a little embarrassed when the class finds out it's his birthday and wants to know his age:

My age came up in class today, because Gretchen [the department secretary] came in with a donut with a candle in it, and everybody had to know how old I was, so that felt strange. I really didn't want them to know, in a way. . . . I said, "Well, how old do you think I am?" and they all [tried to guess]. I said, "Nobody's guessed it yet." Thirty and 29 and 28. Finally somebody said 27. Somebody said 22 [laughs] I forget who that was.

Meredith, 28, says she used to share Mike's concerns:

I used to be afraid of that so much. I never was sure how to deal with that, [with] being so close to them in age in some ways, of sharing so much of their culture. And yet, I'm supposed to be the person in control, or the authority figure, so how do I—I mean, 'cause I share so much with them, how do I become an authority figure?

Now, though, with a little experience, Meredith says she's more "comfortable" with the situation. Often, in fact, she sees the relative closeness in age as a positive factor:

Somehow that becomes a way that I deal with the class, by talking about—I mean, I'm aware that there's this age, there's this ten-year [age difference], but . . . we share the same culture in some ways [and] I bring that out into the open.

As Meredith's experience suggests, it often takes time for young TAs to adapt to their new roles and establish comfortable relationships with students. For most, the crucial issue is authority—or more precisely, their sense of their own authority. In this respect, Peter and Mike are typical of many new teachers—as was Meredith in the beginning. They don't yet *feel* the authority they've been given, so they try to act it out in ways that feel false even to them. In the process, what they lose is the chance to relate easily with students, the chance to use their youth and shared culture to advantage in their teaching.

Not all TAs, of course, struggle equally with these problems. Alex, for instance, seems to regard age as a non-issue. He never brings it up in conversations with me, nor does he give the impression of feeling, at 27, uncomfortably close in age to his students. At one point, when his students invite him to a drinking party, Alex gracefully declines, joking that one thing he doesn't need is to get arrested for contributing to the delinquency of a minor. For the most part, he manages to maintain this friendly but distanced relationship with his students, often calling upon his own student experience, still fresh in his mind, to help him understand their point of view.

Why is Alex apparently able to deal with this situation that his peers find so vexing? Frankly, I can't explain—though the "apparently" I've inserted in that sentence hints at one possible perspective. Perhaps Alex *does* feel the same tensions that Peter, Mike, and Meredith feel, but he simply doesn't talk about them openly. This would be in keeping with what I know of Alex—or rather, with what I don't know. Of the five TAs I talked with, Alex is clearly the most private, the least likely to share confidences about his teaching or his personal life. When I speculate that he may feel tensions that he doesn't acknowledge, it's quite possible that I'm only projecting onto him the tensions I myself would feel. On the other hand, I'm aware that Alex has been bothered by stomach problems this semester, and though he later tells me he thinks they were caused by financial worries, I can't help wondering if his teaching contributes to his stress. If so, what does that say about his "apparently" easy-going manner?

With Keith, who shares some of Alex's self-assurance, I am much less likely to speculate about hidden tensions. For one thing, Keith himself admits to such tensions from time to time. He may not worry about student/teacher relationships as much as some of his colleagues do, but he clearly sees in them the potential for a certain awkwardness. This semester Keith, like Mike, is teaching the "Business and Technical Writing" class, and he knows he will be dealing with a different cohort of students than in first-year composition—but he could hardly have anticipated the awkward situation that arises when he discovers that one of his students, a senior English major, has just enrolled late in a graduate class Keith himself is taking.

When Keith tells me about this situation, I imagine how intensely uncomfortable Mike, or Meredith, or even I might feel in it. Amazingly, though, Keith seems relatively nonplussed. Although he was a little nervous when he first noticed that one of his students was an English major, his only reaction to finding the same student in his graduate literature class is to feel more pressure to perform as a student in that class. As he puts it:

Well my first reaction to him was interesting, I think, when I found out that he was an English major, because I thought, "Oh-oh, here's somebody who might keep me honest, you know" [laughing] . . . [But] he told me later he was more of an English major by default, because he had been here long enough to get a degree, and it just turned out that he happened to have enough credits in English to do it [laughing]. So I dunno, I relaxed a little bit in how I viewed him as a student, but then I see him in the same class I'm taking, for some reason suddenly I felt I had to perform better in the class.

When Keith talks to this student a little later, he realizes the student is more uncomfortable than he is. After that, he never mentions the situation again.

Although I'm surprised and impressed by Keith's equanimity in this potentially awkward situation, in retrospect, I can see how his experience has prepared him for it. First, as an athlete and weight trainer, Keith is used to being perceived as a role model and authority figure among younger peers. Second, though he is only 26, he has served as house advisor for two student groups—his undergraduate fraternity brothers last year, and a group of international high school exchange students this year—and in both these situations he has learned to draw boundaries, to negotiate a comfortable distance between himself and those he lives with. Now, in the classroom, Keith is drawing on all this experience to both establish his own authority and construct positive relationships with his students. Negotiations that are difficult for some of his peers come to him more easily as a result of his past experience.

## The Gendered Teacher

Another aspect of Keith's experience that prepares him to draw clear boundaries is the fact of his sexual orientation. As a gay male in a homophobic society, Keith has learned to keep his personal life private. Just recently, though, he's come out more publicly, and in one of our earliest interviews he talks with me about that experience. My notes—there was no recorder present—summarize the conversation this way:

*[Keith] tells me about sitting at the table of the Gay and Lesbian Students Association at the Activities Fair—how hard that was, how scary. Already, he says, one student has dropped his class because of that. A friend. [The student] said it was because he didn't want to take a class with a friend, but Keith says something [the fellow] had said earlier,*

*months ago, made him realize it was really because Keith is gay. He talks about the looks he gets, sitting at the table, how fraternity brothers come by, and one will stop and talk while the other skitters away as quickly as possible.*

*I ask if this is the first time he's "come out" in this community and he says yes, and he's scared to death. Couldn't sleep the night before. Couldn't eat breakfast. Deb and Meredith came by to talk, he says. He had asked them to, afraid no one else would. And they were angry at the looks and comments he was getting from other students. I ask if others stopped at the table. No—only a few faculty he already knew. People tell us it's important, he says. Even if no one stops, it helps others to see us there. And he believes that. You get all negative comments at first, he's been told, and the positive comes later. It's not my problem, he says. It's theirs. That's true, I say, and you know it's true, but it must be terribly hard anyway, because your feelings may be different. He nods agreement.*

Actually, this early conversation is one of the few in which Keith refers directly to any aspect of his personal life. Aside from one inter-view late in the semester, when he evokes his experience as a gay male to explain how he handles issues of cultural diversity in his teaching, the only other time he refers directly to this aspect of his personal life is when I bring it up, asking him if he'll be involved in Coming Out Week activities. For the most part, he won't, he says, because he's so busy this semester. But he did agree to be a guest speaker in a fellow TA's class:

> She was worried about them attacking me, and I told her that I've heard every name in the book and it's better because— What would be worse [is] if they all just sit there like this [folding arms and leaning back] and not say a word. If they don't like it and they want to complain, great, we have a discussion going.

As we go on to talk about the subject, though, Keith admits he is not always so confident. He was especially nervous, he says, about coming out to his fraternity brothers—the students for whom he served as house advisor last year. And though the subject has not come up with his "Business and Technical Writing" students,

> I'm sure someday that will, in one way or another, become an issue with my teaching, too. That's probably inevitable. Somebody will decide they don't want to have "some fucking fag" teaching the class [laughs] . . . But I doubt they would, anyone would ever say that to my face. . . . The people in the fraternity who I know are the most upset—at worst they give me a cold shoulder and hurry along their way. . . . I try not to think too much about it, 'cause some things about it really do bother me, get me upset.

Although I never sense, in the course of our regular interviews, that Keith's sexual orientation affects his relationships with students, Keith himself, I realize later, may well feel otherwise. One thing he confides, after the interviews have ended, is the fear he sometimes feels walking alone at night on campus. Working late in his TA office, a basement room with large windows at ground level, he will draw the curtains, aware that for certain students—those fraternity brothers who would never say anything to his face, for instance—the opportunity to accost him as he leaves the building alone might prove too great a temptation to resist.

Like Keith, Meredith is well aware of the need to draw clear boundaries between herself and her students. In the past, she says, she has had a tendency to obscure such boundaries, to become "enmeshed" in her students' lives. But gradually she is learning to keep a little distance.

One place Meredith feels that need for distance is in the physical layout of the classroom. Before classes started this semester, she had gone to check out her classrooms, to claim the space in advance, as it were, and see how it might affect her teaching. Last year, she had disliked the setup of one room, seeing it as one source of problems she experienced in the "power structure" of the class. This year, she was dismayed to see she was given another similar room:

> When I walked in, I thought, "Oh, no, another table!" And then I decided how to make the best of it. But I figured out, I think I figured out what it is. When I had this table in 102, I didn't have any space that was my own, because they were just everywhere, and they were on both sides of me, like right next to me. . . . And there was no way to use the board because no matter—there were boards everywhere but no matter which board you used, somebody would have to turn their neck around. . . . And I didn't have my own space so I thought that—That was the classroom that I felt more uneasy about because it seemed like they were, that I lost a little bit more of the control than I meant to. [laughs] I mean it sort of eased into this real familiar thing, which was OK; it wasn't terrible, but it was a real uneasy feeling all the way through. So when I looked at this room I thought, "OK, what I'm gonna do is—" I counted the chairs, to see if all the chairs could fit around three sides of the table so that the whole front part of the table would be my territory and then I could use the board, so I'd have the whole board and that one table that would be my space. And that way it might be kind of a happy medium.

In some ways, Meredith's awareness of distance as a literal, physical issue, is shared by the other TAs. Keith, for instance, mentions an instance in which he held his ground on an issue involving an imposing, but not necessarily hostile, basketball player:

> I had students come in on Monday in my 10:00 class who heard that there was an assignment on Friday, but one guy, he's really tall, I don't know if he tries to intimidate people, but walks up, gets very close and looks down, and he said, "Can I get that memo assignment." I just said, "No" [laughs]. "Well, why not?" "It's a minor assignment—you can't make those up"—and left. And I glanced back and he was still standing there looking at me. That felt good 'cause I—I don't know why but last year I had the tendency to cave in too many times and want to be everybody's friend and keep them all happy.

To compare this instance of perceived physical intimidation with another narrated by Meredith, however, is to see the gendered nature of student/teacher relationships. In this instance, which also occurs at the end of class, a male student comes up to challenge Meredith about an F she has given him:

> I can't remember what he said as much as how I felt, because he was, his body was, just his body, the way—you know what I'm talking about? It just felt like this male presence. It felt like that's what he was doing because he was interrupting me, and at one point he said something like, "Let's get this straight, now." And I thought back on it, and I thought, if I had had—you know how you always think of what you want to say after—if I had had the presence of mind when he said that I would have said, "No—I'm the one who says, 'Let's get this straight.' You're forgetting who's the teacher"—but it just went past me. . . . There were two other people in the room, too, while this was going on—one woman and a guy—and that helped me that they were there, because I knew that they knew that this guy had really blown it, you know, and that I had to stand up to him, and that if I didn't stand up to him then that was gonna destroy my credibility in front of them, too. . . .

After she leaves the class, Meredith finds herself dwelling on this incident all that evening. But the next morning she gets up and writes out what she's feeling in a "letter" to the student:

> This is the kind of thing that used to happen, it would take me a couple of days to recover from. And it affected me that night, but by the next morning . . . I just wrote on there, "I gave you an F because you are a fuck-up [laughs], and a fuck-up has to face justice." And I just called him everything in the book and then I realized that it was—so much of it was about being [physically threatened]. I mean, that's what it felt like to me, you know: "Let's

get this straight." It's like [he's] in control and [he's] gonna say—
He finally had to admit that I had power but it was— The gall of
the guy to come up and even challenge it in the first place was
what—I mean, how could he not think that he deserved an F?

In these instances, both Keith and Meredith hold their ground with
their students, claiming the classroom as their own professional space.
But when I compare these situations in my mind, the contrasting
images I see are telling ones: In one scene, an athletic male TA con-
gratulates himself for not "caving in," as the student who challenged
him quietly leaves the classroom. In the other, a soft-spoken female TA
sits alone at her computer, furiously typing into it all the pent-up anger
and powerlessness she still feels. There are, of course, dramatic ironies
here. One irony is that this same male TA, late at night in his office,
shares Meredith's vulnerability. The other is that Meredith, as she
holds her ground, is learning to claim her own strength.

———————

Of course power struggles between students and teachers are not
always fraught with gender implications. But I could not help noticing,
as the TAs told me their stories, how often gender seemed to play a
role of some kind. In some cases, as in Meredith's story, gender factors
can create or exacerbate tension in obvious ways. In others, the gender
implications may be less obvious, and they may be mixed with other
personal issues.

For Alex, the gender issue never comes up explicitly. Even early in
the semester, when a woman in his class twice makes remarks that
seem designed to provoke male attention, Alex chooses to downplay
their sexual implications, writing off the incidents as mere awkward
moments to be gotten past as quickly as possible. After the first of
those incidents, in which the young woman responds unexpectedly to
Alex's suggestion that the students introduce themselves by telling
"their most embarrassing moment," Alex draws the following conclu-
sion:

That's one of the dangers of asking for an embarrassing moment.
Some might actually come out and say something that truly, you
know, should have been kept to themselves.

The rhetorical move Alex makes here—that move of stepping back to
generalize about a topic he's been discussing—is one that I've noticed
him making before. Often, his generalizations sound like "advice to

new teachers"—as in this passage, where he talks about Glenn, his recalcitrant former student:

> It's that whole idea—don't get personally involved. You get involved, you're a part of these people's lives for three hours a week, and even more when they're doing their homework, but you can't help but feel some sort of failure because this person isn't doing well.... Anyone—to be honest with you, anyone who doesn't feel that, I don't think can be a good teacher. If you cannot be somewhat involved with your students, and concerned with your students, and concerned about your success or unsuccess with the student, you can't really be there for them.

For the most part, Alex is able to take his own advice, balancing a genuine concern for his students with a wise and appropriate distance. But I think of one situation in which his balance is a little shaky. It is near the end of the semester, and Alex is talking about a student he's worried about:

> There's this one guy that was having problems, and he just kinda like disappeared in the beginning of November and hasn't dropped, and he's handed in only one paper, and I have no choice but to give him an F, and I feel really horrible about that, but it's like, "Why didn't you at least call me and let me know what's going on so that I can at least do something for you?" [laughs] I never understand that. I said, I impressed that upon them, or thought I did, to say, "If you're gonna be absent, call me. If you don't want to feel like talking to me, call the English office to leave a note in my box. At least I'll know what's going on."

When I ask if the student might have dropped out of school, Alex says he hasn't. Alex has seen him on campus, as have some of the other students.

> Oh, and he needed help on his writing, too, and I wanted him to come down to my office, but he never made it. What can you do? Those are one of those, Oh well, chalk it up [laughs]. Try to.

Oh, well, chalk it up. This is a phrase I've heard before from Alex. It's one of the things about his attitude I find myself calling "healthy"—in contrast to some of the guilt and frustration I hear some of the other TAs wrestling with, in contrast to some of the same destructive emotions I often feel within me. When I ask Alex how he attains such a perspective on his students, he says, "'Cause it's out of my control." And it is, of course. It's always out of our control. As I listen to Alex, I sometimes get the feeling that we're in some kind of twelve-step program for teachers. He recites the litany, and I listen enviously, wishing I were as far into recovery as he seems to be. But at the same time, something in me once again doesn't quite trust what Alex is saying. Something in me wants to get inside his head and see if he's really following the program he says he is.

Why, I wonder, do I have such a hard time taking Alex at his word? Is it really so surprising that a young teacher could achieve, without apparent effort, that rare balance of care and distance that all good teachers aim for? Well, yes, I guess I do find it surprising. For new teachers, it seems to me, are particularly vulnerable to the emotional claims made by their students. So close to those students in age, so full of ideals, so unsure of their own authority, so beset by the stressful demands of a new job, a hectic schedule, an unsettled personal life—these young TAs all seem far more vulnerable than experienced teachers like me. So if I still have trouble negotiating the emotional aspects of teaching, surely they do as well. Surely.

Still, I'm willing to concede that some handle it better than others. "I suppose it's just a function of personality," I say to Alex. It's a throwaway line, but he picks it up:

> It could be. I try to make every effort to help the students. But with him not showing up at all, he can't— See, I feel more sympathy for him than I do that girl that's missed ten classes.

Hmmm. At this point, my ears perk up again. This student who has missed over ten classes is one Alex has mentioned earlier. In a conference, he had warned her that her grade was in danger. Being sick was one thing, but "skipping out, that's different." Now, because the student has missed so many classes, he's considering giving her a D:

> She's the only one in my two classes that I have that crisis with in a way. I want to give her a D in the class to maybe slap her in the face and say, "Hey, wake up honey." But I also don't want to be punitive. I want to say, "Well, your writing is average, here's your C." I haven't decided what I'm gonna do. That's one of those ARRGH—don't know.

As he goes on, he contrasts this student with the one who "disappeared." This woman, he says, gets no sympathy

> 'cause she had the chance and she had the choice, and it was in her control. She could come to class. She could say, "No, I'm not gonna go home early this weekend; I'm gonna stay and go to class Friday." Instead, she said, "I'm gonna blow off class and go home."

When I ask if he's sure this is what she did, Alex says,

> Yeah, I know, I know. I don't want to go stereotyping people but she's a sorority girl and she's rich. One of the ones with the deep

tan in the middle of winter and "Oh honey, hi," kiss-kiss type—
oof—and I know she goes home because she lives in—[At this
point Alex interrupts himself, realizes he's confusing this girl with
her friend, then goes on.] She wanted to do a paper; she did a
paper comparing her summer cabin to her winter home, and how
the summer cabin is so much better [here he imitates her voice]—
and I just know she—'cause most of the time she misses it's either
on a Friday, because she left early, or a Monday, because she stayed
longer. She's always there on Wednesday, never misses Wednesday, and I just know it, so. . .

What's the difference between these two students Alex mentions—the
one who cut so many classes and the one who disappeared? Both
needed to work on their writing. Both apparently had other agendas
of their own. And yet one of the students Alex feels "horrible" about
grading, while the other he's tempted to "punish" with a D. Is gender
a factor in these different reactions? Has this female student pushed
some buttons for Alex that the male student managed to avoid? Or is
her wealth more significant than her gender? When I wonder about
this, in an early draft of this manuscript, both Alex and Mike offer
comments in the margin. First Alex:

> I guess what ruffles my skirt is [the factor] of economics. The one has the
> ability to take classes with little financial difficulty while the other works.
> And to have school paid for and to squander it irks me. It could be
> jealousy and probably is, but that's just one of those emotional spices, I
> guess.

Mike, a friend of Alex's since undergraduate school, has more to add:

> I think people like Alex and myself feel more sympathy/empathy for the
> ones who "give up." I might be tempted to see the male as an aspect of
> myself—lost and having given up on school. Alex may see it as when he
> lacked direction. Too, there are feelings you get about a student's b.s. She
> was there to give him the b.s. The other guy just disappeared. Maybe if
> he'd been there making excuses, Alex would have no sympathy for him
> either.

Looking back, it's easy to imagine that all of these factors were present
in the situation Alex describes. At the time, though, he doesn't seem to
be aware of them. And in some ways, I find I'm reassured by this: Alex
is, after all, not so different from me: his teaching can be affected by
personal issues like these. On the other hand, Alex's tendency, at the
time of our interview, to downplay the personal dimension of his
relationships with his students makes me realize how strong the pressure is for all of us to suppress or deny that personal element.

## Class in the Classroom

One reason I originally suspect gender might be a factor in Alex's response to the frequently absent sorority girl is the fact that I hear similar responses from other male TAs I have talked to. For instance, one situation Peter describes involves another young woman from a wealthy suburb I'll call Blue Hills. When he first mentions Mimi, at the beginning of the semester, it is in answer to my question about whether he has yet noticed any students in particular. There is one, he says, who is "a lot different from the rest"—an animated, talkative young woman who comes to mind because

> she's so terribly different, you know, as far as an outlook in class, and she's a lot more challenging, I think. I think that she will say what's on her mind if something comes to her mind that she wants to talk about. Some of the people in the class, I think, tend to be a lot more reserved, and I guess that does not surprise me necessarily. I'm that way in school, too, you know, when I'm in a class—at least before, I would be very shy, and not say much at all.

As I listen to Peter talk about Mimi, I think I sense some tension in his voice, tension that he is not at this point ready to acknowledge. Later, more of this tension will emerge as Peter compares students like this one, who come from wealthy backgrounds, to the typical student at our university:

> You know, sure, a lot of them are from Blue Hills, and they know they're from Blue Hills and they walk like they're from Blue Hills, they talk like they're from that town, you know, they drive cars that say they're from that town, they dress like they're from that town, and then you've got little Jane Smith, little Jane Olson or whatever, from the middle of North Dakota, who comes in and starts talking [in her journal] about "I can see why people commit suicide. Just at this university for example, people are treated like numbers. Hurry up and wait, hurry up and wait. What's your student number, what's your student number, I don't care about your name."

When Mimi misses class one week, it's clear that Peter is irritated by her excuses:

> Mimi called, and she said, "Yeah I was sick for like three"—she missed three class periods running, in a row, and she said, "Yeah, I was really sick" [imitates her cough] and I'm just, I felt like saying, "Please, don't even try the theatrics," 'cause I had seen her walking on campus, while I was driving, and I know that's kind of cheating in a way, but I did see her, I can't deny it, and it kinda

bugs me when they think that they're pulling something over my eyes, pulling the wool over my eyes.

Later, without mentioning Mimi by name, Peter comments:

I don't care if they're sick. If they're sick, they're sick, I get sick too, just like everyone else, but I don't like it when they miss three classes running and don't bother to call; then it bugs me, and I feel like then I'm going on this ride and I'm the choo-choo.

By Week 13, Peter's irritation at Mimi and her friend Jen, who are often whispering in class, has escalated. When he finds a piece of scratch paper they have been passing notes on, he's so angry he unloads on the department chair, whom he happens to run into after class:

And then there was a lot of talking going on with Mimi and Jen in that part of the room and it was kind of aggravating but I didn't call 'em on it, but after the class and I picked this up, I was so irritated that I had to talk to somebody, so I proceeded to bend Marcia's ear for the next hour and twenty minutes.... We talked about emotional development of students, and what seemed, the attention span that they seem to have is so short, and the concept of entertaining versus teaching, and things like that.... It was a good conversation. I was ready to go to the computer center and just start writing out reams on ... my whole feeling about this ... and how I felt like I was pretty much, might as well be talking to the ocean or something instead of these students.

Like Meredith, Peter uses writing to vent his emotions—emotions prompted by feelings of powerlessness as a teacher. In this case, I suspect that Peter's anger is not directed personally at Mimi, but at the kind of student she represents. But what *does* Mimi represent for Peter? At first, as I say, I assumed that it had something to do with gender. And perhaps it does—I cannot help noticing, for instance, the gendered nature of the discourse he finds so irritating:

I just thought this was really disheartening to see, that, certainly they have other things on their minds, and I understand that, but ... when I see stuff like this, and I see their journal entries—both of these students have journal entries almost filled, Mimi has hers filled with things about sororities, and "I'm really sorry that I couldn't make it to your class today, but at least I was able to meet with my Big Sis tonight," and then I wrote in the margin, "I'm glad to see you have your priorities straight." I'm getting tired of seeing that in these journals, even though it's a wide-open avenue for them to express writing; it's almost consistently with Mimi on sororities, and with Jen it's almost consistently about her boyfriend who's a beet farmer with a mobile phone. And somebody else who's also in that row is writing very reflective essays about, about anything from death and dying to snow and why there is snow and things like—I mean at least that shows me that there's something up there, there is some grey matter that's functioning, but when I see this kind of stuff it's kinda like, why are you here? Why don't you just go back to high school and take it all over again and then maybe come back.

But when I offer this interpretation, in an early draft of this chapter, not only Peter but Mike and Alex resist my reading: *"Why is this necessarily a gender issue?"* Mike asks in the margin. Although he thinks that *"the gender issue is present somehow,"* Mike speculates that the more important issue may be anti-Greek sentiment: *"Might he not say the same thing, in the same tone, about a 'frat boy'?"*

Peter himself offers a different, but perhaps related, interpretation:

> *I think my response [to Mimi and her friend] was based more on the background of wealth and that these two women didn't seem interested in carving something out of the wood they're apparently made of. I get irritated with people who coast on gifts bestowed upon them because of the luck/money they were born with. I want to see them work, especially when they need to work to improve. They are, after all, in college. Why? For looks?*

Although Peter is aware that his relations with students are sometimes fraught with subtle gender complications, he clearly sees this particular situation as having more to do with economic status than with gender. It reminds him, in fact, of a conflict with a male student he had consulted me about last year. That student was also from a privileged background, and although Peter hadn't mentioned it at the time, he's pretty sure now that his awareness of that background accounted in part for his impatience with the student's behavior.

When I think about what Peter says now, it makes sense. It confirms Alex's impression that economic status was an issue in his relationship with the two students described earlier, and it confirms something a colleague had said when he read an early draft of this chapter. As English teachers, after all, we are well aware of our status in a wealth-oriented society. When we see students from privileged backgrounds shunning the gifts we have worked hard to earn, it rankles. And it may rankle even more for TAs who have gone deep into debt to finance their graduate education. Still, I wonder why I didn't notice at first the extent to which economic status might be an issue in these relationships. Is it, as Peter suspects, because I've forgotten what it's like to be a graduate student? It's true—I'm now tenured, a homeowner, secure. Meanwhile Peter works summers as a janitor to keep himself in grad school and Alex literally worries himself sick spending money he doesn't have. In retrospect, I suspect Peter is right. I have forgotten the extent to which differences in economic status can affect our relationships with our students. What else, I wonder, have I forgotten along the way?

## Family Matters

Another personal factor that sometimes finds its way into these TAs' teaching is the family drama—the complex set of scripts upon which they have collaborated with their parents, their siblings, their partners. Although most of these scripts remain invisible to me as I talk with the TAs about their teaching, there is one that the TA himself calls to my attention.

It is the end of our project, and Keith has read through the transcripts of our interviews. When I ask if he's noticed any patterns or themes, he answers immediately: "My mother. I can't believe how often she comes up."

When he says it, I'm a little surprised. Although Keith's mother is a prominent character in his personal script—a character he sometimes evokes for us in an amusing, Jonathan Winters-style voice—I have not given that much attention to her place in our conversations. Keith didn't either at first, he says, but then he started to notice a pattern: When his mother makes an appearance in our interview transcripts, it's a clear sign he's feeling less confident than even he admits. Her voice, he says, is the voice of his own insecurity.

Once he says this, it makes sense to me. At the beginning of the semester, when Keith is preparing to make a quick trip home before classes begin, he anticipates what his mother will say about this new course he's teaching:

> She says, "You're teaching 'Business and Technical Writing'? You don't know anything about that!" And the same kind of thoughts maybe last summer went through my head that, "What do I know about teaching composition?"

Almost always, his comments are affectionate, ironic—as in this early reference, when he talks about how little he got done on his thesis on Edith Wharton over the summer:

> I thought I was gonna get all these Wharton books read. Didn't do that either. I need to have somebody who's cracking the whip and keeping me on schedule. But I don't want my mother coming up here [laughs].

Still, sometimes there's an edge in his references, as in this comment, from that same early interview:

> I'll enjoy being home, though, because my mother will insist—she'll look at the syllabus and the things I scribble and she'll [say], "You can't teach these kids how to write; you can't even write yourself. Look at that mistake!" [laughs]

At midterm, when he's sick but feeling guilty about missing classes, Keith says it's his mother's fault: "When we were kids she would never let us stay home unless we were definitely really, really sick. She always said the best thing for a cold is to get out and do something." And at the very end, when he's about to hand out course evaluations, he muses:

> The last few weeks before I hand the course evaluations I start worrying, and I always—I'm getting better about handling worry, because I see what it's done to my mother. . . . It's such an internalized thing for her that she has to worry. She's worried if she's not worrying. And I'm getting better about just figuring if it's nothing I can change the outcome of right now, I won't even think about it, but the last few weeks before I hand out the course evaluations, I wonder what they're gonna say.

Still, despite these allusions, Keith's mother isn't that much a presence in his narratives—at least not literally. Sometimes, though, I sense that Keith may see her in some of the female students he talks about, and I wonder if Keith himself is aware of that possibility.

One instance that brings this thought to my mind occurs during the first week of classes. Although I did not tape-record this part of our conversation, my interview notes testify to an interesting juxtaposition in our conversation:

> *Before taping, Keith gives me his journal tape—on microtape—and we go over to Twamley [cafeteria] for lunch. Already in the line he's telling me he gets memos [from his students] tomorrow and that his mother, a secretary for years, will see them when he reads them. When we sit down to eat, he says he's already been intimidated by one student. "How big is he?" I ask. "She's a 50 year old secretary who's been working at the University 24 years," he says. We talk about this a little, about his going home for Labor Day weekend.*

As the semester goes on, Keith finds that this older student, far from criticizing his teaching, is one of his greatest fans. When he learns, from his teaching supervisor, that she has praised his teaching, he is obviously pleased. But at the same time, there is another female student in his class who is driving him crazy.

This other student—whom he describes first as "ugly," then as "abrasive" and "disruptive"—also comes to Keith's attention very early in the semester, when he tells the class they will be pairing up for interviews and introducing each other to the class.

> It was really quiet and she says, "Do they tell you GTAs to do this in every one of your damn composition courses?" And I said, "No they don't *tell* us to do it, but I'm telling you to do it" [laughs]. And she said, "Well what purpose does it serve?" and I said, "You get to know the other people in the class, even though you might not want to, and I get to know you, even though I might not want to." I don't know if I was in a bad mood at the moment or what but just, her response seemed like sort of a challenge to my authority and I guess—I might have overreacted in saying that, that's not something I usually say in class.

Hearing Keith tell of this incident, I am reminded of another dialogue he has described—a dialogue that took place when he showed his mother some of his students' papers:

> The first thing she says [is] "They can't spell" and . . . "They're ending their sentences with prepositions, and they're beginning their sentences with conjunctions." And then I showed her, after a few minutes of this, one of the transparencies I use. It says, "Grammar Rules," and there's one column "Grammar Rules to Remember," [and another] "Grammar Rules to Forget." And beginning your sentences with conjunctions and ending your sentences with prepositions are in the "To Forget" column. "How can you do that?" [she asked]. "Well, you go over to duplicating services, you hand it in, they make a transparency" [laughs].

Now, hearing echoes of this same mild sarcasm in the voice he uses to chastise his "abrasive" student, I wonder if Keith may be using, in the classroom, strategies for asserting authority that he has learned unconsciously from sparring with his mother. The extent to which these strategies are gender specific—used on female students rather than on men—I can't say, but I do notice that in another situation a similar pattern occurs.

In this situation, Keith is recalling a student from last year's 101 class:

> I remember the one problem student I had. She was from [an out of state city]. And we did the interview thing the first day of class, where you interview someone, introduce them to the class. So she made sure to give the interviewer details on her wealthy background. From the very beginning she set herself off as being different, probably better, I think is what she was trying to do, and I had them do some freewriting on what they expected from the class 'cause I was sort of curious . . . and most of them had no idea

what to expect from the class, but she said, "I expect *you* to make this class interesting" [laughs]. And she was a really good writer but halfway through the semester she just decided to quit coming to class and didn't hand in rough drafts, and then I remember after grades were turned in, as I was packing to leave to go home for Christmas, she called me and asked if she could turn her final drafts in. I told her if she wanted to mail them to me to look at, that would be fine but grades had already been turned in so it was a bit late [laughs].

When I ask Keith why he remembers this woman, he says,

She was loud, for one thing. . . . This summer there were a lot of students [in my Air Force Base extension class] who spoke up very freely. But she was pushy. She would speak up and interrupt other students or me, which finally I had to talk to her after class [about] and she quit doing that, but she didn't have much respect for what other students were saying, particularly when we were talking about some political or social kind of issue and somebody was expressing what might be considered the typical [local] kid's viewpoint that she didn't agree with. Even if I didn't agree with it, you don't try to make the person feel bad or insult them for their point of view.

What is interesting about this student is how closely she resembles others the male TAs have commented on. She's from out of state, wealthy, outspoken, aggressive. She has missed several classes and now wants to turn her papers in late. With the others, I thought I sensed a bit of sexual tension, heightened, I later realized, by an awareness of class difference. With Keith, the issue is still one of authority, but the gender dynamic is clearly different. If family history is a key element in Keith's response to students, might it be present, though less visible, in the other TAs as well?

———

Unlike Keith, Mike rarely mentions his family in our conversations. And yet sometimes, as we talk, I sense that his family is lurking in the background. Largely, this is a matter of tone of voice. As Mike talks about his students, I keep hearing a tone that I can only call "parental." I'm well aware that such a tone need not be learned in the family. The whole culture of school is permeated with just such a tone. And yet I wonder: How much of our attitude toward students, the language we use when we speak to and about them, is shaped by the language our own parents used with us?

In Mike's case, I don't notice the parental tone at first, though as the semester progresses, I become more and more aware of it. What I do notice almost immediately, however, is Mike's desire to see himself in his students. After meeting his "Business and Technical Writing" class for the first time, he comments that these students seem more "serious" than his 101 students did:

> They've all been through courses, and . . . the newness and the strangeness of taking a class, and being in college has kinda worn off, and now they're in the class and they're looking at it in terms—I just feel a lot closer connection to them because that's, I mean they're sitting there in class, and I'm seeing myself there, you know.

As Mike goes on to characterize his students, he draws parallels with his own experience:

> I mean, that's how I approach class. You go in there and you sit there and you've got that—I don't know how to describe it, but that knowledge of what a class and what a course is and how to learn and . . . so forth. And also caring about what you're doing, you know, feeling like you have more of a personal connection to the course than I think the students had in 101 or even 102.

In some respects, Mike is like the parent who sees in his child a new and better version of himself—a successor who will avoid his mistakes and fulfill his dreams. What this means, of course, is that he is headed for disappointment. For although the young men and women he sees in this 200-level class may be more committed to college than 101 students are, they are still a long way from the serious graduate student Mike has become.

Although Mike does not explicitly use the parent metaphor (I notice that Alex and Peter do), he often seems to adopt a parental voice when he speaks of or to his students. In the following passage, for instance, he compares his students to irresponsible children:

> I haven't had assignment sheets this semester, except for the first time, and as childish as it may be to have to write all this down—I mean, I repeat it several times anyway—I'm just gonna have to do that, because people forget.

When I ask Mike why he considers it "childish" to give out assignment sheets, he makes a rhetorical move that all of us recognize:

> Well . . . I mean to have to have it written down is very, very [pause] juvenile somehow. I guess I sort of expect students, or hope that students will take the attitude toward their schoolwork that when something is due [you] find out everything that's done,

and you write the notes down, and you've got all that, and the questions might be a clarification of something, or might be an extension beyond what I cover, but it shouldn't be the basic things like how many pages is it supposed to be. When somebody comes to me and says, "How many pages is it supposed to be?" or whatever, things like this that I've talked about before, it's like, well I know this person was sitting there in the room looking at me when I said this, and they wrote something down so . . . where does it go? . . . I'm not talking about the assignment sheet in terms of how to understand what it is you're supposed to write, but I'm talking about just the basics, in terms of when it's due and so forth and so on. I mean, when I was a student, I knew that stuff, I mean I just had it, even if it wasn't, if it wasn't on an assignment sheet, . . . I mean people would say, "Well such and such is on this date," whatever, I mean it was there in my notebook, I knew when these things were.

What is interesting about this passage is its nostalgic flavor: "When I was a student . . . " Mike intones, as if his own student days are long past. Though he's obviously referring to his days as an undergraduate, the fact remains that Mike is much less likely than, say, Alex or Keith to see his less-than-ideal self in his students. Later, he'll offer an explanation for this:

> *Part of the problem is that I flunked out as an undergraduate, and my self-confidence was/is pretty low as a result. My fear of slipping up again colors my expectations of my students.*

For Mike, to "measure up" as a student is to be serious, committed, and responsible—to be the kind of student he became only *after* he "flunked out." Similarly, to measure up as a teacher is to be expert, knowledgeable, always in control. But perhaps the most formidable aspect of Mike's demanding code, for both himself and his students, is the injunction not to "take it personally."

---

Actually, "taking it personally" is not so much something to avoid—in fact, Mike believes it is only natural—but rather something to contain. In this respect it's a little like the primal sex drive or original sin: a force that, unacknowledged and undisciplined, can wreak havoc in the classroom. For his own part, Mike has anticipated what happens when teachers and students take things personally, and he has chosen to deal with it this way:

> In my syllabus I said, . . . "Everybody knows you're supposed to go to class, everybody knows you're supposed to turn your papers in on time. I'm not here to harass you about stuff." I said, "If you turn it in late or you don't show up, I'm not gonna take it personally," which is not true [laughs], but I said, "I'm not gonna take it personally." I said, "Likewise, of course, it's gonna have some effect on your grade. I hope when this applies, this situation applies to you, *you* will not take it personally or get offended." You know, I was trying to set up this whole thing like, "Look it's your decision and it's not gonna be, you know, I wanna be able to take the hard line and still be a nice person." That's what it comes down to.

As he tells me about what he has written in his syllabus, I can almost anticipate what will happen. Here once again is the parent, lecturing his unruly teenagers about the responsibilities of being an adult. "This is our family contract," Mike seems to be saying. But the students aren't listening. When they turn in the first assignment, just one week later, Mike is disappointed to see that some have done only a slapdash job:

> You sort of expect brilliant work, and it's depressing when people just write down a list, you know, . . . it's hard not to take it personally, that somebody would do that and like, "Well, so what am I doing, am I just wasting my time up here?"

On the one hand, Mike knows that it's "all teaching and it's all part of the course." But then there is "that personal element" that makes him long to say to them, "Fine, you don't care about. . . the work that I give you and, you know, it's meaningless or something, or you're just trying to get away with it, you think I'm stupid or something."

For Mike, it seems, "that personal element" gets into teaching in both positive and negative ways. In one sense it's an important element of his teaching philosophy, as demonstrated by how often he talks about the need, for both students and teachers, to make "personal connections" that allow them to learn. In another sense, though, "taking it personally" means trouble—which is why Mike gets so tangled up when he talks about it.

> The whole reason I said that I don't, won't take it personally is because I want them to be trapped by that in a way. So you can't take it personally if I give you bad grades, right? And if you think I'm, you know, if you're gonna take it personally then you've gotta assume that giving me that stuff means I take it personally, which means you get bad grades—or something, you know. I think they're smart enough to figure that out. I was thinking about Elbow when I did that. . . . I was thinking about that when I wrote that section, you know, that's sort of, that's sort of subterfuge in a

way, putting a statement in there like that. But it's like, it's sorta like, we all recognize it, and for some reason I felt like saying it indirectly rather than saying it directly like that. I wondered about that. I think everybody knows what's going on. I think they know I know what's going on.

According to Mike, what underlies the literal message of his syllabus is a subtle subtext: Let's face it, we all take it personally: you take it personally when I give you a bad grade, and I take it personally when you do shoddy work. We don't dare say that directly, but if we acknowledge it in coded terms, we have a better chance of controlling it. As he says,

On one level it's just a transaction, you know. It's like give and take, action and reaction, you don't show up and you're not participating, you don't get the points. . . . I'm trying to put the system between me and them so that I don't take it personally or something, you know. Like well, put it in terms of action and reaction and scientific formula and so forth and it's not, the part of it that makes me, that offends me, is suddenly, you know, that makes it impersonal or something. There is that, you know, so it's weird, there's a couple of things going on there.

To evoke the parent analogy again, Mike's confusion on this subject reflects a parent's confusion about how to deal with a recalcitrant child. On the one hand, he doesn't want to "guilt" the students, but on the other, he thinks they need to be more responsible. To avoid the personal, he sets up a "system," like a set of house rules, that he hopes will mitigate the personal element. But Mike's system pales beside the other system that is already working inside him: the moral system of "should's" and "ought's" that pervades his language and constructs his relationships with his students in ways he may be unaware of.

### Voices of Guilt and Judgment

The situation in which I first begin to posit conflicting systems in Mike's thinking occurs during the fifth week of classes, when he is 10 minutes late arriving for his 8 a.m. class. Because I am out of town when it happens, I hear about it first not in our regular interview, but in a long journal narrative Mike writes out and gives to me afterward. As I read the narrative, I am struck by its unusual tone. In some ways, it reads more like a legal deposition than a journal entry.

*I arrived in class at 8:15, and was met by three students who told me that everyone was gone. "Oh really?" I said, hoping to sound curious and amused, though I was at first panicked, then angry. I proceeded to*

*the classroom followed by these students, and found that it was true; all but five or six students had left.*

*I felt like this was a culmination of all the fears that my class was out of control (or rather, that I was out of control) I'd been having since the beginning of the semester. Or rather, I felt like I <u>should</u> feel this, or expected to feel this, but realized (as I always have when feeling this way this semester) that it was not that serious; I am not out of control, nor is my class. Once I realized this I was still a little nervous, but somehow relieved. Somehow this was my opportunity to show myself that I was not out of control, as well as showing my class this (whether they needed to see it or I needed to think they saw it!). I guess I felt (and feel to a certain extent) that they see me as an inexperienced teacher (because I am young and joke around and am obviously at times nervous, but mostly because I see myself as inexperienced).*

Those reading the narrative now will notice how slight an incident this is. Which of us hasn't overslept, come late to class, felt our authority undermined by a stupid blunder on our part? But it isn't just guilt Mike feels, it's something more: "I was angry the more I thought of it," Mike writes.

*I was angry, because I took it personally. Here we are back at this one again; how can we not take it personally? So, I do, and I knew that when I wrote [that statement] in my syllabus, but I guess I am continually surprised that I do. I was also embarrassed, because the rest of my students who were there . . . I felt like they were in league with the other students, and that if I had not shown up when I did, they'd have left too. Anyway, I got through class well, after making a few remarks about the relative intelligence of "the others'" actions, and went back to my office.*

*One of my students showed up to turn in his paper, and asked what we had done in class. "Good question," I said sarcastically, some of my anger leaking through.*

*"Hey man, you were late!" This accompanied by a meaningful look at his watch. I am sure my face was as pale as his paper. "Yes," I said, "I was." I was so angry, I was not sure what I was going to say. I decided nothing would be gained by confronting him now; I wanted to deal with it all at once the next class. I told him what was due Tuesday, and accepted his paper. I did not say he would or would not get credit.*

*After he left, I thought about it, and decided I was not going to go out of my way in the slightest to help him over the semester. I already know that I have to be selective about how much energy I devote to different students, and I decided he had just earned himself minimum energy status. I was still angry.*

It's easy to speculate about why Mike is so angry at this student. He is probably angry at himself for being late to class, for losing the slim power advantage he may have had until then. But what interests me most is the language Mike uses to express his anger—language that becomes more moralistic as he continues to write:

> *I called Academic Affairs to check the official policy about late instructors; there is none. I began to think about what my students thought about my policy and school policy. I had told them that class started technically at 8:05. Point number two: I had told them that as I lived twenty miles out, I might have trouble making it in some days [a reference to our rugged winters]. I also told them that I would call them personally if class was canceled if there was time, or at least call the office. Point number three: they believe (as all students do) that after ten minutes, they can leave if the instructor has not shown up. Conclusions: I had arrived ten minutes late (in the room), I had not canceled class, therefore class could be assumed to be happening. Add to this the fact that those who had left had not turned in or left papers behind, and I began to feel a sense of righteous indignation.*

As Mike comments further on this incident—how he felt about it at the time and how he chose to deal with it—his language continues in this moralistic/judgmental vein: he considers "penalizing" the students who were absent and says he feels "justified" in doing so; he gives them a little speech the next class day in which he tells them what they "should have" done, and feels that he pulls it off "without sounding vindictive." Afterward, he says, "They all knew they had done something wrong."

But Mike doesn't reserve his moral language for his students alone:

> *Six or seven of them got up later and told me they'd have their drafts to me by noon, and were so embarrassed that I felt a little guilty. Clearly some had been swayed by others (many of my "good" students had left), and I suddenly remembered how easy it was to do that. I also remembered that the times I had done it, I had expected some sort of retribution, and in some way I think they were relieved I had addressed it this way.*

Guilt, goodness, vindication, retribution—these seem odd words to apply to such an unremarkable incident. And there may be an element of conscious irony in Mike's use of such language here. Still, this is, from Mike's perspective, a "very significant episode." What is at stake in his mind is his professional authority, an authority that feels so fragile, so tenuous, at this point in his young career, that he must reinforce it with strong moral language. *"I feel I did the right thing by taking the hard line,"* he writes in his journal.

> *This event allowed me to confront what I thought was their perception of weakness in me, but which in reality may be only my fear of inadequacy in a new environment. It could also be a mixture of both, I don't know. But I feel much more confident about that class now, for whatever reason.*

## Our Students, Ourselves

While all five TAs speak, at one time or another, of seeing themselves in their students, I am interested in the different ways they construct their student selves. With Mike, for instance, that self seems less the student he is or was than some idealized version of the perfect student that he still berates himself for not being. With Meredith, I can see more correspondence between the students she seems drawn to-ward—the "rebels," she sometimes calls them—and the person she is, or is becoming. And with Peter, I often think that I'm seeing both at once—a tendency to seek in his students some idealized vision that he himself could never fulfill, plus an almost opposite tendency to iden-tify, perhaps over-identify, with those who may feel insecure in the "impersonal" academic environment.

———————

For Meredith, the true aim of education is self-knowledge, and in an effort to lead her 101 students toward that goal, she has arranged, as I explained earlier, to show the film *The Breakfast Club*. Although she realizes that her students may not be familiar with the movie (this is the point when she begins to realize that a generation gap may be opening), she believes they will still find it interesting and provocative. Whether or not they identify with the teenagers in the story—the jock, the nerd, the popular girl, the neurotic—Meredith is gambling that they will recognize aspects of themselves in the characters and can thus be led to examine their own experience in light of the movie.

Of course it is just as possible that they will *project* their experience *onto* the characters in the movie, reading those characters through the lens of their own experience. This is not something Meredith brings up in our interviews (though I suspect she is well aware of it), but it is something that occurs to me as I listen to her talk about her students. And it keeps coming back to me again and again as I think about my own relationship with Meredith.

As we'll see in the chapters that follow, Meredith sees herself as a "rebel" among English teachers—a teacher who rejects what she thinks she "should" be doing (that is, teaching grammar, teaching argument) in favor of an agenda she sees as far more important. Having heard her characterize herself as a rebel in several situations, I am interested when I notice that the students she singles out for notice in her composition classes seem to have a rebellious side to them as well.

The most obvious instance of this is a young woman Meredith talks about in our Week 4 interview:

> I have one girl who's real rebellious. I remember sitting in my class the week before, and one of the days I was sitting on the desk and she sat in the front row and she was just staring at me, you know, that really blank stare, and everything comes through the eyes, but there's no expression. And every time I looked at her it was like—it was like somebody was hitting me in the face or something. And I couldn't look at her, because if I looked at her I felt like it was the evil eye or something [laughs] so I had to look past the front row, or I couldn't talk. So her paper was all about how she did exactly what she wanted to do, never did what other people expected her to do, and she had—her story was about when she went to this private [Catholic] boarding school, and they tried to sneak through this tunnel or something to steal some food in the middle of night and they got caught. So I told her I was a Catholic and said, "So you must have had nuns there," and she said, "Yeah, they slapped me in the face." She started talking about being hit by the nuns and how terrible that was.

When Meredith makes suggestions for how this student can improve her paper—what detail she can add, what further episodes she can narrate—she senses that the student is resisting her:

> She's already prepared to not do anything I say. . . . She said, "Well I just wrote what I thought." She said, "Everybody else probably just told you what they thought you wanted to hear." . . . So I don't know—but just this terrible look she had on her face, it was just awful, I just wanted to get rid of that look 'cause I can't stand to go through the whole semester with her looking at me like that.

When I ask Meredith what she wants for this student, she searches for an answer:

> Well [her draft] was very—I wanted it more—I wanted it to have more of her voice in it. It was like she was walking around in a circle trying to see if she could say what she wanted to say, or—it wasn't very focused. I mean, if she can get beyond the rebellion . . .

As the semester progresses, Meredith mentions this student often, never using her name but rather offering metonymic descriptions that I immediately recognize:

> Oh that girl, by the way, the one that the nun slapped her in the face? She missed class on Thursday, but Deb said she came in to the office, and she had left a note.

The fact that the student had left a note is something that "impresses" Meredith. This, and the fact that she "talks a lot in class now" gives Meredith reason to believe that she is making progress with the student. It is at this point too that she answers a question I had posed about the value of teaching personal writing. What she wants for this student, she says, has "nothing to do with writing." What she wants is for the student to realize that "it's not necessary to rebel against every figure of authority, that you can actually enjoy what you're doing in a class without having to rebel against the teacher." As she says it, I seem to hear a double meaning in her words. It's as if she's talking about herself as well as this student.

Actually, this isn't the only time I have this particular reaction. Over the course of the semester, six or seven of Meredith's students make repeated appearances in our conversations, and with many of them I sense that Meredith has made a personal connection of some kind.

There is, for instance, a woman student around Meredith's own age, whom she describes as "a really good writer" but "scared to death" about coming back to school. When the woman's doctor husband criticized a draft she had written, Meredith was outraged: "Well, I better not get into this, contradict her husband or I'll get in trouble," she tells herself.

> But I can't really imagine that he could have been right, because what I read before—I don't know, I mean it already gets me kind of irritated 'cause how much do doctors know about writing? I've had pre-med students before, and I've worked for doctors . . .

Later, when she puts this student in a group with two other students, Meredith is impressed at how well the older woman handles the situation: "It wasn't as though she thought that she was so much better than them," Meredith says—at which point I recall something she has told me earlier. It is a story about her grandmother, who always cautioned Meredith as a child not to "get the big head": "Now you're very smart," she would say to Meredith, "but don't ever get the big head. Don't ever think you're better than anybody else."

Among the others in Meredith's cast of frequently mentioned characters are a wide variety of students who evoke for me faint traces of the Meredith I know: a possibly dyslexic student who worries Meredith at first but later turns out to be very articulate in class; a female student from last year who resisted Meredith's assignment, insisting on doing the paper "her own way"; another, somewhat older, student, this time a male, trying to break free from a past involvement with drugs; a "jock" who wrote a thoughtful paper about having beaten up a kid in high school because he was pressured by his peers to do so; a cheerful underachiever who wants to take her class again in the spring, even though he's getting a C and could obviously be doing better; a male student who wrote a powerful first paper about leaving home for the first time, and then got frustrated when she tried to push him to claim his "voice" in subsequent papers. Even the student she found physically threatening, the male student she calls the "fuck-up" in her journal, reappears later in the semester, at which time he has "suddenly become very diligent," written some good papers, changed his whole attitude toward the class.

To say that Meredith may identify with these students, that she may see herself, or parts of herself in all of them, may be speculation—but it's not *just* speculation. In her writing during the teaching seminar, Meredith explored this topic again and again. In this respect she resembles Mike, who uses writing about his teaching as a kind of controlling strategy. As both Meredith and Mike narrate their versions of an event, for me and for themselves, they construct a point of view on the matter, an argument they can use later when confronting their students about it. But while Mike's writing tends to be somewhat ad hoc—a response designed to suit the particular occasion—Meredith's seems to emerge from something larger, from a growing understanding of herself as both a person and a teacher.

During the eighth week of classes, something happens with Meredith that prompts her to talk with me about this understanding. The incident itself involves two confrontations—the first with a friend, the second with a student—and though both issues seem to be fairly minor matters, I sense that Meredith experiences them as something more than this:

> *Libby:* I guess I'm thinking—this doesn't sound, as you narrate it, it doesn't sound like a particularly extraordinary set of circumstances, and yet somehow it came together for you today as a—as a thing.
>
> *Meredith:* As a thing, yeah. Well, I make everything into a thing. I'm trying to stop doing that. I was gonna come in today and tell you how much more *even* my teaching is [laughs], how much less I worry about it, which is all true, except for this little incident. I mean, I'm upset now because I'm upset at [my friend]. But what I'm trying to say is that I've started to confront people instead of letting them walk all over me.
>
> *Libby:* In your personal life and your teaching life.
>
> *Meredith:* Yeah. And because those things run together so much . . .

When I ask what she had planned to tell me before this incident came up, Meredith explains:

> I was writing some stuff this morning and I thought, "It's funny how I feel detached from my students." And I thought, "Well that's bad, maybe that's bad," and then I thought, "No, it's not bad. I'm still informal, it's not that I've become formal again, I'm still informal, I mean I'm still relaxed, but I don't feel so caught up with it, I don't feel so [pause] enmeshed or something." I thought that was good.

Later in the semester, Meredith comments once more about the progress she's made in this direction. This time, she's talking about responding to papers—about the way she sometimes feels "obligated" to give personal responses and how she's learned to "detach" when this happens. What has enabled her, I ask, to detach emotionally?

> Well, I think I finally just saw that it wasn't very good for me. And [pause] part of it is the whole, where I've come to in . . . my overall life. But trying not to always take responsibility for everything, whether it's for them or for other people, not thinking I have to solve everybody's problems, and thinking more in terms of trying to fix myself instead of everybody else.

---

Like Meredith, Peter often mentions particular students in our conversations. But when he's frustrated, like most of us, he tends to speak of students in the aggregate:

> I must confess that early this week, especially after Tuesday's first class when so many people missed, I was having kind of an attitude, not toward the students but like to Brad [another TA] and my confidants. To my students I was very civil, I'm trying not to show them when I'm irritated, unless I really, really am irritated at them and it's their fault, they're not paying attention or whatever, then I might pull them aside, but I'm not gonna, I'm trying to learn from last year's mistakes, and I think it's working so far. But I was saying to Brad . . . I said, "When these students call me and say, 'I missed your class, what did you talk about today?' I feel like saying 'Blank you,' but I don't, I tell them, 'Well, we did such and so,' but I really feel like, 'You come to class and find out, buddy, don't call me afterwards and make me talk to you on the phone for twenty minutes.'"

The fact that Peter is aware of the anger and frustration he's feeling is reassuring—and yet I have to wonder how successfully he has concealed these feelings from his students. My own experience suggests that our students have sensitive antennae that allow them to pick up on our anger, sometimes well before we do. Because Peter understands that his own fear and nervousness may be significant factors here, he seems better placed to control them than some new teachers would be. Yet as we talk throughout the semester, it seems to me that, despite his apparent understanding of the problem, Peter is often still struggling to control the anger he feels.

One way he controls it—or re-directs it, at any rate—is by blaming himself for the problems:

> It does kind of hurt me, or not really hurt me, but it makes me think, it makes me wonder what I'm doing wrong when I see students crashed out on their desk, you know, head on their arm or something, or looking away, looking at their nails or something. They're obviously bored, and I'm wondering how I can rectify that and make them more interested.

He is particularly worried that he is boring his students and comments frequently on things he does in class to keep their interest and attention. By the eighth week of the semester, in fact, he has become almost obsessed with "the boredom factor":

> I've been trying a lot of different things this year that I haven't done last year to keep them interested, to keep them going, 'cause I don't want them sitting there and being passive, and I'm not taking roll, and I've still been maintaining attendance. Yesterday I had five gone—or was it six?—that was quite a few from the 8:00 class, normally there's not that many gone. So at least I have that going for me—they're still showing up. But I'm looking at them and I'm seeing them just kind of with their eyes closed and they're waving back and forth, or they've got this look on their face where they're like this close to having their eyes closed, and I keep thinking, "What am I doing that's wrong?"

As Peter casts about for ways to understand and address the "boredom factor," I occasionally find myself swept up in the currents of his dismay. Instead of listening, as I usually do, I begin to offer suggestions: "Have you tried this? How about that?" But the more I try to build Peter's confidence, the less he seems able to hear me. As he shuttles back and forth between blaming himself and blaming his students for the problems he sees in his classes, he comes up with a dozen different ways of addressing the problem—most of which make perfect sense to me, but none of which may have an effect on what now seems to me the larger problem: Peter's lack of confidence.

### The Harsh Light of Criticism

Where Peter's lack of confidence originates, I don't know. No doubt it's complicated. But Peter himself attributes some of it to an incident that occurred in his first year of teaching—a situation in which he was criticized by his peers for the way he handled a plagiarism case. As he writes long afterward:

> *I think part of my nervousness with becoming comfortable with my role as teacher was due to Ian's holding me up to the harsh light of his (and the other grad students') criticism. It was trial by fire, and I got toasted enough to remember it through much, if not all, of my teaching days at UND.*

The incident Peter refers to here is one I'm familiar with. He had told me about it at the time, in the heat of his anger and frustration, and then had written about it in the teaching seminar. His reflective essay, "How to Make a Brown-Eyed TA Blue," was clearly intended as both catharsis and public response to what he felt had been an unfair indictment of him by his peers in that group. Although I would like to reprint the complete essay, letting Peter tell his own story, the final version seems to have gotten lost somewhere along the way. What I do have is my memory and Peter's first draft, plus some additional comments he offered later, as this manuscript was in progress.

What had happened, it seems, was this: Peter had caught a student plagiarizing—turning in a paper that had been written by her roommate. He referred the student to me, I made a recommendation regarding appropriate penalty, and he made a decision based on that recommendation. As it turned out, the plagiarizer's roommate was in another new TA's class, and when that TA, Ian, was pulled into the situation, he called Peter at home to criticize the way he had handled it. As Peter tells the story in the first draft of his narrative:

> *Both of us were greenhorns at this pedagogy stuff. [Ian] called me after the Director had put the word out wondering if another TA had the same paper turned in. When we started talking, however, he mentioned that I should not be tormenting this poor kid over something as trivial as a lifted paper. I was dumbstruck. . . . When I responded by saying that I was consulting the Director on this issue, he told me that I was stupid to go to The Authorities about this, and wondered why I didn't have enough sense to take care of it on my own.*

When Peter first told me about Ian's reaction, I too had been dumbstruck. Why would one new teacher ridicule another for asking advice from someone more experienced? What could Ian possibly be thinking? But according to Peter, it wasn't just Ian who turned against him:

> The rest of the TAs didn't offer much support for me, and many seemed to side with the TA who had criticized my handling of the situation. I felt very prominently like an outcast within the group of new teachers—and this was only three months into the program.

Given Peter's sense of betrayal, the depth of feeling brought out in this essay, I was not surprised when he brought up this incident again in our very first interview.

That interview took place the week before classes began in the fall. The workshop for new TAs was in progress, and the acting comp director had asked Peter and some other returning TAs to speak about their first-year experience. What Peter had spoken about was this plagiarism incident and its aftermath. As he describes it:

> I talked about the plagiarism thing, and you wouldn't believe the response I got. They start talking—all these first-year TAs—and some of them, Brad remarked, looked like they could use a valium [laughs] when they started talking about the plagiarism thing. And Samantha [one of the new TAs] said something about, "Well, with plagiarism" she prefers "not to mention it because then it won't enter their minds." And I said, "That's like not telling a teenager about sex!" . . . I just thought, "No, that's not gonna wash with me, I can't operate that way"—and then we had this big discussion about plagiarism police and Keith had some good things to say about that. . . . But I let it be known that I was not very pleased about the way I was kinda cornered about that last year . . . and I said I think I should be able to have the right as a brand new TA to consult my mentor about such a situation, [without being] coerced and ridiculed about my decision. . . . I mean, I was in the limelight about that for a long time and I didn't like it. . . . It was kinda messy for a while, but I don't look back upon that with any bitterness with the exception of the way I was treated by my peers.

Later in the same interview, when Peter talks about the policies he's set up this semester, he mentions this incident yet again:

> I was just so sick of that whole plagiarism affair because of the way it got blown up by the other TAs, the factional fighting, if you will, and I got kinda caught in the cross hairs, . . . they just sighted right on me, and I don't want to go through that again. I just want to be left alone when it comes to plagiarism, and if I have to deal with it I'll just deal with it when the time comes, and I think I was just a little bit bitter about the whole experience.

At the time, I remember thinking that Peter was more than "just a little bit bitter" about this experience, but I didn't fully appreciate how much it had affected him until he brought it up yet again when he read through this manuscript. For him, it wasn't just this single episode but the whole competitive atmosphere among the new TA group that contributed to his feelings of nervousness and insecurity. As he wrote on the last page of the manuscript:

> I am struck by the dysfunctional aspect of my group. I think we were all peaking out of our respective closets in [the teaching seminar], waiting for someone to slip and fall out so we could all laugh at the presumptuous slob. We were rivals, not friends, by and large, waiting for a cannibalistic opportunity. If someone slipped, then we'd know what they were and what we were.

Reading Peter's comments now, I find myself wondering: Was the atmosphere in the new TA group really so competitive that year? Did other TAs feel it as strongly as Peter did? It's hard for me to know, of course. This is not the kind of thing they are likely to talk about with me. But I wouldn't be surprised if others did share Peter's perception. After all, those of us who have been through graduate school know something about competition among peers. We may even have felt the chilling effect a peer's criticism can have on our teaching. Still, some teachers seem more vulnerable to criticism than others, and I suspect Peter is one of these. Of course there's a positive side to that vulnerability, too. Sometimes I think it is Peter's lack of confidence that enables him to empathize with the students in his class who are struggling. Peter is, after all, a caring teacher—one who truly wants to help his students become better writers, better people. His problems occur, it seems to me, when he invests so much of himself in his students that he blurs the boundaries between them and himself.

## Blurred Boundaries

I hear the strongest instances of Peter's tendency to blur those boundaries in a conversation we have around midsemester. At the time, Peter is feeling particularly stressed out. His entire week has been devoted to student conferences—always an exhausting experience. In addition, his personal life, he says, has been a roller coaster of ups and downs this week, and to top it off he has been reading student journals—over 400 pages of them—and he is feeling utterly burned out, emotionally drained.

When I ask him if he feels he has to read everything the students write in the journals, Peter says:

> I didn't at first, until I started coming across entries that said, "I hate my life. I love my shotgun," you know, and I thought, "Oh God!" and I'm starting to read all of these because I was worried that I would miss an entry in there about some poor student who doesn't have a friend up here, and they might kind of relate to their comp instructor 'cause their comp instructor might appear to be quasi-cool to them, and approachable, and here they are writing in this journal that I'll be reading, about how their life sucks or something—'cause I actually ran into about two different entries like that—not that blatant, but they were serious enough for me to call them up on it, and call them up right then and there, not wait.

When I inquire further, I learn that Peter was so concerned about both of these students that he did in fact call them at home:

> Yes. At home. And granted those journal entries are dated like a week or two ago, and [the students are] still hanging around, of course, [but] I called 'em up on it and I said, "You know, I just noticed that in your journal entries you seemed a little bit unhappy or depressed," I said, "I just wanted to ask you if everything's OK, you know, and if not, do you want to talk about it." I said, "If you don't want to talk about it with me, that's OK, but maybe we could set you up with somebody who you might like to talk about it with."

In this case, Peter draws an explicit parallel between his students and himself. In his first year of college, he went into a serious depression after being "dumped" by his girlfriend:

> I was like a basket case, walking around going, "I hate my life," and a sociology instructor caught me on that. I was taking a test and there was some weird question, and I said something about how life seems to have no meaning when you get dropped by someone you love or something, and . . . he wrote—he didn't even talk to me on the phone or see me in person; he handed this test back to me and wrote there, "I really think you ought to see somebody over there . . . in the Counseling Center. It's free, please make an appointment." . . . And so I did and that—it took me a while but it kinda snapped me out of it, and I just want these students to know that we have stuff available to them.

Although this particular incident involves two female students—a factor that puts me on "gender alert"—I know that it is not only his female students that Peter shows concern for. In that same week, for instance, he says he has been "kicking himself" for handling badly a conference situation in which he critiqued one male student's paper in front of another. This time, Peter makes no reference to his own experience, but because I know how anxious he is about his own writing and how sensitive he is to the criticisms of his peers, I can see that once again he may be identifying, even overidentifying, with his student.

To some extent, this is typical behavior for Peter. He is, as he himself admits, "hypersensitive" to the reactions of others. But this week, with his own emotions so close to the surface, he is especially vulnerable. It seems that any student paper that treats emotional subjects can trigger an emotional response from him:

> I just didn't know if I could handle somebody breaking down and crying in front of me because it's been hell week for me anyway, and my emotions have been up high and then they've been way, way down, and then they've kind of leveled off again. And I was afraid if they did it, then I'd start doing it, and then what would happen? . . . I didn't want to make them think of me as being so moody that I would do that. I mean, I would be fighting it tooth and nail not to show the emotion, but I was worried that I would be able to stick it out, because of all the other crap that happened to me this week.

I have said that Peter is "a more vulnerable teacher than some." At first—when I was just planning this study—I asked myself whether this made him "atypical." Was Peter more emotional, more insecure than most new teachers, I wondered? Was he too much an anomaly in this group?

When I admitted my uncertainty in an early draft, Peter offered this response:

> *The bit about me being the odd TA, the anomaly, was an eyebrow-raising experience for me. Am I really that different from the others? Maybe they just don't allow their facades to be lowered?*

Actually, I think Peter may be right. I had said, in that first draft, that I wanted his perspective because in him I could see, in exaggerated form, the personal element I had learned to control in my own teaching, adding with more uncertainty, *"Or perhaps 'control' is not the right word. Might 'suppress' work as well? 'Hide,' 'Deny'?"* Perhaps I wanted the ambiguity. Perhaps I just wasn't sure. At any rate, Alex knew what I was getting at, and what he wrote in the margin confirms Peter's suspicion that he's not all that different after all:

> *How about accept and name and therefore co-exist? It's the same in a sense with me. Naming is power. If I can just see it for what it is—nervousness, insecurity, whatever—I can manage to adjust to it. You can never control it—harken back to every first day of the semester. It is the*

*recognition and acceptance of what that fear is that lets us go on. That and the addiction of teaching, the successes, even if there are only a few.*

## Conclusion

I began this chapter talking about boundaries—the boundaries new teachers draw, or try to draw, or fail to draw, or blur, when they try to strike a balance between the personal and the professional. For these TAs, who are well aware of the tensions inherent in this issue, there is no simple answer to the question of where or how to draw boundaries. On the one hand, it seems perfectly reasonable to say, "Don't take teaching personally. Don't get upset if your students cut class. Don't overreact to students who bug you. Don't get involved in their lives." On the other hand, we cannot deny who we are and what we feel as teachers.

Although I admire those who seem to know, instinctively, how to integrate their personal and professional selves, I seem to be the kind of teacher who struggles continually with this problem. The image that comes to mind is one I see in the optometrist's office. I am seated in the leather chair, chin resting on the concave plate, peering into the ocular instrument. "See the blips?" the optometrist asks. "Yes," I say. "Let me know when they merge in the center." Then, I watch as the tiny blips move in from both sides of my vision. Closer . . . closer . . . Suddenly they have leaped over the center and are headed back out to the periphery. "Wait!" I tell the eye doctor. "I missed that." So we do it again. And again. And never once do I see those blips converge, though I know they must, know other patients report that convergence as confidently as I read the top letters on the chart at the end of the room.

What this means for my teaching is something rather complicated—or else it's very simple. Maybe all it means is that I never get the balance right. Maybe none of us do. Still, we need to keep working at it, struggling always to "make teaching personal" without "taking it personally."

# Interchapter:
# Research and the Personal

The personal, we recognize now, is always political. But it works the other way, too. All along I worried about the gender balance in my group of five TAs, the proportion of one woman to four men. All along I asked myself that tough question: Am I perpetuating, through my choice of interview subjects, a culture in which men's voices are heard above women's? There are ways I could answer those questions, but they don't entirely satisfy. For instance, I could take the anti-essential-ist route, argue that balancing gender is simply cosmetic diversity. More important, I might say, is the diversity of attitudes and person-alities among those I did interview. Or I could call attention to the voices that *are* heard here: Meredith's voice, some readers tell me, is the strongest of the five TAs'. And then of course there's mine. But for me, the most powerful argument to make is not really an argument but an explanation. As it happens, the gender imbalance in this interview group reflects the gender imbalance in the new TA cohort that year: two women and ten men. For me, at the time, the imbalance was simply unusual—a reversal of the pattern we had seen in earlier years. As I look back now, though, I'm convinced that this very imbalance engendered—I use that word deliberately—the crucial personal disso-nance that eventually gave rise to this project.

At the time, I was certainly aware of a dissonance in the group—an unusual resistance among the TAs to the work I was asking from them, an unusual level of competition that built up within the group itself. I even ascribed this tension, in part, to the "maleness" of the group. What I didn't see then, but have begun to see since, is that the tension wasn't in the male TAs themselves but in the dynamic that grew up between them and me. There was something about my authority that made them want to challenge it—and something about their air of confidence that irritated me. What ensued was a power struggle I was determined to win—but one I could win only by exchanging some of my authority, my insistence on doing things my way, for some of their confidence, their admission that they were not as sure of themselves as they seemed.

Now, looking back on the teaching seminar, what I see is a situation surprisingly akin to those I have written about in this chapter, a situ-ation fraught with gendered tensions, power struggles, authority conflicts, projection and identification. In the midst of it all, I felt myself drawn toward certain TAs: first Meredith and Mike, in whom I thought I saw some part of myself; then Peter, whose anxieties reminded me of my earliest teaching days. With Keith and Alex, I felt not so much a bond as a kind of fascination. They weren't at all like me, and yet they were serious teachers. I suppose, in some way, they represented selves I would like to invent.

Still, when the project began, I had no close ties to any of the TAs. I felt at ease with these five, liked the work they had done, and they in turn seemed relatively at ease with me. But in the beginning, we hardly knew each other. As the project wore on, though, I felt new bonds and tensions growing between us—bonds and tensions created by the changed circumstances of our relationship: no longer were we simply teacher and student but something richer and more personal. With Alex, as might be expected, there has been the least change. We've remained on cordial terms throughout, but always at a bit of a distance. Mainly, this is because Alex drew implicit boundaries in our interviews. He did not, as did the others, share confidences with me in our conversations, and I chose, for the most part, to respond to the boundaries he erected with a professional reserve of my own. With Mike and Keith, in contrast, I have developed a certain rapport—a rapport that allows me to think of them as friends now, or perhaps younger colleagues. Again, it seemed to be they who established the boundaries of our relationship—in this case boundaries that blurred a little the professional/personal line. With Peter, who takes teaching so personally, I feel less like a colleague than a counselor—or maybe an older sibling. For the most part, I would simply listen as Peter wove talk about teaching in and out of talk about girlfriends, family, and peers in such a way as to defy boundaries altogether. Occasionally, I would share stories of my own with Peter, but I sensed, as I did so, a difference. The stories I told the other TAs were spontaneous, reciprocal, prompted by something in me that wanted to confirm what they were saying. With Peter, my stories had morals, hidden meanings; with him I could never quite shake off the teacher role.

Then there was Meredith, the only woman—and with Meredith it was always complicated. At first, I think we were wary of one another. Something about Meredith's intensity both intrigued and unsettled me, and something about me put her on guard, as well. As we talked, though, almost from the first, we discovered common experience. "Does that make sense?" Meredith would ask me, grasping for language to name a tangled thought. "Yes, yes," I would say, excited, and then I would find myself drawn into what was no longer an interview but a conversation between peers. Eventually, there grew up between us an intimacy of sorts, as of two schoolgirls sharing secrets. Meredith, whose experience has been darker than mine and who has acquired through that experience an uncommon understanding of the complexity of human motives, was attracted to psychological and philosophical questions. It was she, as I've said before, who helped me understand what I wanted to do with this project: "This is your story," she would say when we talked about it. "This is really about you."

At first, I took what she said as a kind of reprimand: You say you're writing about us, but you're not; you don't know us at all; stop pretending you do. She didn't actually say that, but I imagined that she did—and I felt reproached. I had set out, in the beginning, on a noble mission: to speak for those whose voices we don't hear in this profession, to create space in which those voices can be heard. I should have known better, of course: all ethnographers are colonizers. But I guess I hadn't understood it well enough. I wasn't prepared when Meredith phoned, after reading the earliest draft I had written, to say, "I'm not happy with this." I wasn't prepared for the coolness that came into her voice, for the almost audible sound of barriers dropping back down between us. What had happened, of course, is that I had gone public with our conversations—had reassumed my researcher role. And although Meredith had known all along that this was our purpose, had even signed a contract acknowledging that understanding, she hadn't realized how "violated" she would feel.

I guess I hadn't realized it either, though I probably should have. In the course of our conversations, we had blurred the boundaries between the personal and the professional in ways that I found both personally and intellectually stimulating. But then, I was in control. Perhaps for Meredith, the young teacher, the woman just learning to assert her own authority, the blurred boundaries in our relationship were as unsettling, in their way, as the blurred spatial boundaries in her first classroom. To be comfortable with the way the project was unfolding, she would have to assert control over it, just as she had asserted control in that room.

For a while, I thought Meredith and I had resolved the problem. She told me what she didn't like in the draft, and I listened: I made cuts, I revised wording. But in the editing process something besides words disappeared, and I have hated to lose it. What disappeared, for me, was that sense of integration, that sense that somehow, in my conversations with Meredith, I had managed to merge, for an instant, the personal and the professional, had seen the blips converge on the darkened screen.

To achieve such a merger, I have learned, is a tricky business. Always, it seems, we are squinting at one image or the other. Always there are boundaries, yet those boundaries blur and shift before our eyes. Always, we tell ourselves not to take our work personally—yet we must make it personal if we want our work to have meaning.

# 2 Thinking Theoretically

It is the first week of classes, and Keith is talking about his plans for the "Business and Technical Writing" course he is teaching for the first time. What he's looking for, he says, is something to "tie the whole course together with," but he's not sure what this will be:

> I remember in "Problems in Literary Criticism" this summer, Phil Adams [the graduate professor] would always say that all teaching is based on theory. And I didn't always agree with that because, particularly with a new teacher like myself . . . I don't know enough theory to base teaching completely on it. I know bits and pieces of several theories, and I know maybe one or two well enough so I could sit down and explain them clearly to other people, but I don't think I have any one theory down well enough so I can say, "OK, this is what I'm gonna base my teaching on." So I think—I like using a theory, but I don't want that to ever constrict my teaching style because I probably have several theories I'm actually using . . . mixed in with common sense and instinct.

For Keith, as for all these TAs, theory seems to be something alien, something other people do. Even when they "like using theory," as Keith admits he does, they are not entirely comfortable with it. And when they don't like it, when they're not attracted to theoretical discourse, their associations with theory may be even more negative.

In many ways, I'm not surprised by this alienation from theory. Although I have quoted to students that often-repeated line about everyone having a theory, but some just being unaware of it, I, too, have trouble using that word to describe what I think and believe about writing and teaching writing. Instead, I tend to talk more about assumptions, beliefs, understandings—all, not accidentally, in their plural forms. If pressed for a singular noun I will nearly always choose "philosophy" over "theory," and though I've taught for eighteen years now, describing myself as a "composition specialist" for the last twelve of those years, I have never grown entirely comfortable with the concept of "composition theory."

At one point in the course of this project, I actually wrote a little essay about theory. Not an essay, really, but a rant. (See the next interchapter for more on this.) At the time, I saw no connection between that essay and this interview project, but in retrospect, I believe they are closely connected. As I listen to these TAs talk about teaching writing, I realize that they are in fact theorizing constantly, and this realization has led me to understand and accept as theoretical my own reflective thinking about teaching writing.

## Defining Theory

Since I'll be using the term "theory," comfortably now, throughout this chapter, I want to make clear how I'm using it. For me, to theorize is to enter into a conversation about meanings, whether that conversation occurs in the pages of journals, in teacher talk with peers, or in silent internal struggles to resolve conflicting goals and purposes. Whenever we speculate about what writing means, about how we learn it, and about why we teach it in college, we are theorizing, and whenever we act on what we know and believe about writing and teaching, we are acting on theory. In this respect, the five TAs I talked with were often theorizing, whether they would call it that or not.

I recognize, of course, that not everyone will accept my definition of theory. For some, theorizing can only be done in the language of academic discourse. As one early reviewer of this manuscript put it,

> Academic/theoretical discourse is complicated and uncommon because it is writing against the "everyday." It is required to take up a language that is "different" so as to make sense of the "given." The theorist must make sense of the everyday in terms that are not the everyday.

While I appreciate this reader's perspective, I cannot say that I agree with it. First, I would argue that theoretical discourse—like poetic discourse—is not inherently different from "everyday" language. It is different, yes, but its difference doesn't inhere in the language—it inheres in the context. Thus the phrase "make sense," which the reviewer uses above, may be theoretical discourse in one context, communicative discourse in another. Whether to regard it as theoretical may depend as much on the perspective of the listener as on the intentions of the speaker. For instance, in our conversations, as I've already mentioned, Meredith often would end a speculation about teaching with the question "Does that make sense?" to which I might or might not respond, depending on the circumstances. At first, I think I assumed that the phrase was largely phatic in function: a cue to the listener to enter into the conversation, a request for a signal to go on. But at some point, I began to hear Meredith's "Does that make sense?"

a little differently. I began to hear it as meaning making in process: as Meredith struggling toward meaning, inviting me to struggle with her. She was theorizing.

And this raises a second point. For some, discourse counts as theoretical only if it is "new." We speak of making knowledge as if there were a large cultural pot somewhere that we make collective contributions to. If someone has already contributed what we have, it doesn't "count as knowledge." I have trouble with that. For one thing, I wonder who's holding the pot. Who is it who knows it all, who has all the theory? Who gets to say what is new and what is just old hat? What is new to Meredith may not be new to me, it's true. And what's new to me may not be new to the dissatisfied reviewer. But is there nothing new at all here? Perhaps it's just that this reviewer hasn't learned to hear theory in everyday language. After all, isn't that what the canon wars are all about—about our failure to hear certain voices? If we grant that we now read as "poetry" what was once simply "verse," as "literature" what were once only "popular novels," shouldn't we also recognize that "theory" may emerge from nontraditional sources as well?

I'll admit that this wasn't always apparent to me. In the early days of this project, I remember feeling worried that my interviews with the TAs rarely touched on what I saw as "substantive" matters. Although I had made a conscious decision to let them set the agenda for our conversations, I began to notice, as I typed up the transcripts, that those conversations often focused more on the TAs' personal struggles—struggles such as I have described in the preceding chapter—than on the subjects covered in our professional journals.

On the one hand, this didn't bother me too much. I know it is impossible to separate the person from the teacher in me, and it makes sense that the same would be true of others. Besides, what we talked about together almost always seemed important. Still, as my research journal entry of October 10 attests, I was sometimes vaguely uneasy about the content of the interviews:

> *Halfway—not even halfway—through transcribing Meredith's interview, I take a break and take the dog for a walk. So little of this stuff is about writing, I'm thinking. Is it really about teaching at all? After all, I'm not watching them teach, I'm not hearing what they think at the moment of teaching, at the moment of responding to a paper. All I'm getting are the kinds of things it's easy to talk about afterwards.*

I'm not sure what was the source of my concern (Was I afraid the project wouldn't be "publishable"?), but I eventually developed ways of dealing with it. For one thing, I learned to be patient. As the semester wore on and the TAs got more comfortable with me and with themselves, they tended to become more reflective, more inclined to talk openly about what they thought and believed about writing. Also, I allowed myself to venture occasional probes—to raise a question here and there that did not come up "naturally" in our interviews— and those probes often spurred thoughtful responses. Finally, I think I learned to recognize that even in conversations that were not explicitly theoretical, that did not touch on matters having to do with how and why we teach writing, there were often implicit themes and issues that tied right into the ongoing conversations of the profession. By engaging the subject in these conversations—revealing my own doubts, playing "devil's advocate," or offering personal anecdotes from my experience—I would often find that I was prompting incipient theorizing, theorizing that lay just beneath the surface of our conversations, ready to emerge when the occasion presented itself.

## Resisting Theory

One reason I was sensitive to this issue of theory was because of signals from the TAs themselves. Except for Keith, who is clearly intrigued by theory though skeptical about its usefulness at this point in his career, the TAs rarely mention the word "theory" in our interviews, and when they do, it is not in a very positive context. For instance, when I ask Peter, early in our interviews, what he liked about teaching last year, he says:

> Generally just learning by doing. The whole idea of teaching, just mechanically working through the nuts and bolts with them, instead of—you know, there is a time and a place for the theory, I think that there's still a time and a place for theory of teaching and pedagogy in my career . . . but actually getting in there and getting your feet wet and your fingers dirty and scraping around in the mud—that's what it boils down to.

Although Peter does not explain what he means by "theory" here, I suspect from previous conversations that he is referring to what we read in the teaching seminar: Mike Rose's *Lives on the Boundary* (1989); Peter Elbow's *Embracing Contraries* (1986); Anne Gere's *Writing Groups* (1987); and Cy Knoblauch and Lil Brannon's *Rhetorical Traditions and the Teaching of Writing* (1984). The latter, especially, seems to have exasperated Peter—largely because of its academic style—and to have formed his notions of what is meant by "pedagogical theory." Though he pays lip service to it here, commenting that "there is a time and a place for theory," he makes it clear in other contexts that he finds most readings of this sort irrelevant to the "nuts and bolts" of teaching.

While Meredith is more likely than Peter to use the word theory in a positive context, she, too, harbors some negative associations toward it—associations that may derive from the experience of the teaching seminar. At one point, thinking about how she might design a first-year writing course, she begins to imagine a reader-response approach, then stops:

> I don't know. I don't know what— Because now I'm more topic-oriented. . . . I'm more topic-oriented instead of theory-oriented or method-oriented or whatever.

Although "theory" may not be quite the word Meredith wants here—as her immediate substitution of "method" and "whatever" suggests—the fact that it even occurs to her as a possible opposite of "topic" may reveal something about the way she regards it. For Meredith being "topic oriented" seems to mean focusing on the "what" and "why" of writing—questions that she believes are primary; in contrast, being "theory oriented or method oriented or whatever" means focusing on more technical matters, the "how" of writing that she finds much less interesting.

For Mike, too, the word "theory" has negative connotations. Talking about how we learn grammar, he draws an analogy with the different approaches to teaching ESL advocated by two linguists on the faculty:

> I mean we've got two schools: We've got [Professor] Tanner's school which says that theory and intensive language training is what's going to give you your second language, and then there's the [Professor] Jacobs school that says you should learn things in context. And I learned more Spanish in three weeks in Costa Rica and more about the grammar and how to put things together than I would have if I had spent a semester in Spanish 101.

In another context, responding to my question about whether we should try to reach some consensus about how to teach writing, Mike says:

> I think that's our problem—I think we're too order-oriented, I mean . . . we've got to have the answer, writing has to be a science and science has to have the answers and it will explain the universe and we will find out what the truth is, etc. etc. etc. and every time, I think every time that people get this move towards, "Oh, we gotta have a consensus," "Why can't Johnny read," etc. etc. etc., once we move towards this thing we screw it up. We can get close to each other up to a certain point and then we end up with just a mess, and . . . "Here's the new theory, here's the new an-

swer—now everybody, if you're anybody who's a professional, you'd better understand this and apply it in your classroom." I mean, I don't think there's anything wrong with striving for a consensus, but to ask that consensus to be the way that everybody teaches is—I mean it doesn't work for me, it doesn't make sense to me.

In many ways this is an interesting monologue—and I'll return to it later to fill in some of those ellipses. For the moment, all I want to show is how Mike uses the word "theory" here—how he associates it with order, with answers, with science, with truth—but also with what's new and trendy in academic circles. Where did he get that impression, I wonder? Well, I have my suspicions. And they are confirmed when Mike jots in the margins of an early version of this manuscript:

> *This is what we all in that class [the teaching seminar] were rebelling for. The critical discourse seemed to deny the value of personal theorizing.*

From this mix of reactions, I can see that for Mike, as for Peter and Meredith, "theory" is a problematic term. Indeed, for new teachers, "theory" may be so alienating in its language that they want nothing to do with it. This seems to be what Peter and Meredith are saying. And even when it's attractive, as it is to Keith—and to some extent Mike—it may seem so elevated, so idealized, that it is well beyond their ken, or so closely associated with positivistic science that it's not applicable to their work.

## Everyday Theorists

Still, even TAs who resist the word "theory" do think theoretically about teaching. Meredith, for one, acknowledges that fact when she says, at the end of the semester, that she has taught in a manner "consistent with my theory." And Mike, too, turns out to be a serious "everyday theorist." In the conversation quoted above, for instance— the one in which he associates theory with something like academic fashion—Mike demonstrates some of his most impressive theoretical thinking. In an entry in my research log, composed shortly after the interview, I note:

> *Transcribing Mike's Week 13 interview. He seems to have thought more about writing, about what it is and how it's learned, than any of the others. Says he's been doing it since 501 [the teaching seminar]. Things he's thought about:*
>
> > *difference between Comp and Business and Tech*
> > *how one TEACHES writing*

> *the difference between what you've learned and what your grade is*
> *how college courses relate to previous writing courses*
> *connection between writing and reading*
> *what's NOT teachable*
> *how people learn language*
> *connection to foreign languages*
> *connection to speech*
> *what knowledge of grammar tells us*
> *how teachers learn to teach, and improve*
> *that it's all dynamic*
> *the politics of language*
> *power and pedagogy issues*
> *that what works for him may not work for others*
> *relates creative writing to comp*
> *integrates more from other coursework*

Of course, Mike hasn't pulled his ideas together yet, or seen all of their theoretical implications, but he is certainly "thinking theoretically" in this conversation. That is, he is going beyond his own classroom, raising questions about the meaning of our work that all writing teachers eventually face.

Although Keith, Alex, and Peter have also given thought to many of these theoretical questions, they are somewhat less likely than Mike and Meredith to talk explicitly or at length about them. Partly, this may be due to personality. My impression, drawn from reading their teaching journals in the graduate seminar, is that both Mike and Meredith are unusually reflective people, accustomed to engaging in internal dialogues about both personal and professional matters. But personality is only part of the story. Another factor that affects the level of theorizing these teachers do is the extent to which they are comfortable with the course they are teaching.

While none of the TAs could be said to be perfectly comfortable with their courses—perhaps no teacher ever is—it is Mike and Meredith who feel the most dissonance between their own implicit theories and the assumptions underlying the courses they are teaching. It is they, then, who possess the greatest incentive to explore theoretical questions, as a way of resolving that sense of dissonance.

## Dissonant Theorists

What does it mean for teachers to be "comfortable" with the course they are teaching? Essentially, it means that the course "makes sense" to them, that its purposes, methods, and underlying assumptions seem compatible with their experience as writers, their intellectual background, and their ideological commitments.

Experienced teachers will often know right away how they fit with the program—especially in programs where the purposes, methods, and underlying assumptions of writing courses are not only firmly articulated but actually woven into the program through prescribed texts, program guidelines, and in-service workshops. But when teachers are inexperienced, and when program philosophies are only loosely articulated, either by neglect or design, it is harder for teachers to sense their level of compatibility.

For the TAs in this project, the process of sensing their own comfort level is one that has not been easy. In some respects, our program is one of those "loosely articulated" ones. On the one hand, we offer new TAs lots of guidance. They participate in an orientation workshop, a fall practicum, a spring seminar in composition theory; they are invited to attend weekly brown bag discussions and are given a program handbook for teachers. On the other hand, we have defined our courses broadly, in an attempt to make room for a wide variety of pedagogical theories and styles, and that breadth has forced new TAs to construct their own interpretation of the courses. As a result, their notions of what they are expected to teach vary somewhat from one teacher to the next, influenced not only by official program materials but by various other factors, including readings from the teaching seminar, conversations with peers, and conventional wisdom about what constitutes first-year composition. Of all the factors that most influence how these TAs construct the courses they are teaching, though, the most important seem to be their own school experiences and the texts they are asked to use.

## The Program in the Mind

It makes sense, I suppose, that we construct the courses we teach in the image of the courses we have had in the past, yet I am frequently surprised by how powerful those images are. A case in point is the grammar issue. Although our program materials make virtually no mention of teaching grammar, many teachers simply assume that it is part of the package. For instance, Meredith, as I have mentioned before, feels that she is expected to "teach grammar" in the 101 course, though her desultory efforts make clear that she has little faith in the efficacy of such teaching. (Other TAs persist in believing that they are expected to teach "the research paper" in 102, though our program guidelines state only that "students can expect to explore and/or research their subjects before writing" in *all* composition courses.)

It also makes sense that textbooks should exert a strong influence on teachers. Because the text is something teachers use nearly every day, they know it much more intimately than they know the program handbook, the fall workshop materials, or the theoretical readings assigned in the one-semester teaching seminar. Besides, as Bob Connors (1986) has observed, until recently the only "real training" most composition teachers got "came from the rules and tenets found in the textbooks they asked their students to buy" (190). Although most teachers these days get a little more training, programs with limited resources often still rely on textbooks to help new teachers structure their courses. In fact, one reason we chose our 101 textbook was because we thought it offered new teachers such support.

As it turns out, though, even the most supportive textbook can get in the way of the teacher, and when the TAs I talked with felt tension between their implicit theories and those of the course they were teaching, they were most likely to express it in terms of their dissatisfaction with the text. This is not to say that the text is the only source of tension—or even that it is the primary source. As I talked with the TAs, I was always aware that, because I was so closely identified with the program, they might not feel free to express dissatisfaction with aspects of the program I was responsible for. Although I tried hard to invite their candor, expressing openly my own dissatisfactions with the program and assuring them of my interest in their views, I suspect they may have found it convenient, occasionally, to express their theoretical dissonance with the program in terms of disagreement with the anonymous textbook authors. And in some cases, they may even have understated that disagreement.

### The Well-Dressed Theorist

Because Alex never actually *initiated* conversations about matters I have called theoretical—general issues having to do with what writing is, how we learn it, and why we teach it—I assumed, in the beginning, that he was less theoretically oriented than some of the other TAs. To some extent, this may be true, I think, but a few weeks into the semester, when I decide to test my assumption by raising some of these questions myself, I discover that Alex does have ideas on these subjects. He just hasn't brought them up in our interviews.

In the last chapter, I spoke of the particular perspective Alex brings to his relationships with students—a perspective that struck me as "healthy" or perhaps just unusually mature. In many ways, he brings that same perspective to the course he is teaching. Although he may internalize stress about some things (I keep remembering those stomach problems), nothing he says gives me reason to believe that he has really serious conflicts with the 101 course or with the composition program as he has constructed it.

Last year, Alex had resisted the course a little—but that was largely because he had negative associations with composition from his high school and early college background. In high school, he says, "I hated English, 'cause it was mostly grammar and I hated grammar." In college he took first-year English and got an A, but his memories are hardly positive:

> I don't remember much about it, to be honest. I don't even remember the papers that I wrote, I don't think I even have them anymore. You got 'em, you looked at the grade and ppfft—tossed. The only thing I remember is once you handed in the paper that was it—there was no revision. She said, "You're gonna stand on how you do right here, right now, and that's it." I mean, she says, "You can learn from my comments and the mistakes on this page, but you have to apply that to the next paper." And that's the one thing I remember most about it.

It was only in creative writing classes that Alex was able to rediscover the enthusiasm for writing that he had felt as a boy writing heroic fantasy stories to accompany his "Dungeons and Dragons" games.

Given his experience, it is little wonder that Alex arrived at graduate school with a firm conviction that composition and creative writing are two different animals, and a belief that what he had come to understand about writing through his creative writing courses would be in conflict with the composition course he was assigned to teach. In the first semester practicum, Alex was one of several TAs, all interested in creative writing, who resisted the notion that comp and creative writing could be closely related:

> We wanted to be creative writing teachers and had not reconciled ourselves to composition and did not really want to accept what composition was. I think that was my problem. But the more that I got into it—I guess it started in 102 more than 101 'cause too much was going on to sit and think about it—but the more I went through 102 the more I started thinking, "No, there isn't much difference in the writing."

Actually, the approach to writing that Alex seems to espouse is much more linear and skills-oriented than our program is designed to be. Where he picked up that approach, I don't know (his friend Mike says he's just a "rules-oriented person") but I do recognize the language Alex uses, and I suspect that those composition classes he hated may have influenced him more than he realizes:

> You need that beginning, you need to start off slow, and work your way and get comfortable and then move up to the next stage. I kinda told them it's like, OK, first I had to learn how to tell a story. Next I had to learn how to write dialogue. Then I had to learn how to mix dialogue in with writing a story. Then I had to learn about all the elements that go into a story. Said, that's the same process. First you're gonna learn how to express your ideas. Then you're gonna have to learn how to express your ideas in a well-reasoned fashion. You know, one point leads to another to another to another to your conclusion. Then you're gonna have to mix different subject matters with different writing strategies; it's all this sort of progressive thing; it's kinda like learning—the one I hate to use but I use anyway is the drinking beer. The only way you can learn how much beer you can drink is by drinking too much. And then as you get older, you get to recognize these stages of inebriation. And it's the same with writing. The more you write, the more you recognize different stages.

Having reconciled his views of composition and creative writing, Alex is now relatively comfortable with the 101 course. Although he does not always agree with the textbook and thinks its language is unnecessarily academic at times, he finds its assignments reasonable and likes the way it treats writing as a "building process." Though he says he hasn't always made the best use of the text, he thinks he can use it better in the future:

> I have to sit down and try to use . . . materials that [the text] has provided. I might not do the assignment the exact way that they have it stated, but I can probably use their examples to suit my purpose better than I have. That's one of the things I'm gonna work on.

For Alex, the bottom line is always simple: "If you can present your ideas clearly, that's all that counts. I mean, that's what writing is, I think." As he tells his students,

> If you're gonna be a professional, you're gonna need to . . . write letters, write memos. If you're gonna be anything in the sciences you're gonna need to write papers. You're gonna have to tell everybody what you're doing. And you're gonna have to be able to do that clearly and concisely.

When I ask Alex how he would respond to students who argue that they don't need Comp I, then, since they can learn these things in "Business and Technical Writing," he replies:

> I tell them about my experience [in] creative writing, that even though I have had years, five and six years of writing workshops, I'm still learning, and I had my composition way back as a freshman undergrad too, and it's just, it's the repetition. The more you write the more you recognize your mistakes, and the more you learn how to correct them at the creation stage. Whereas . . . if you jump right into 209, you're gonna be competing with students who went through and have had this, these two semesters or one semester of getting used to the process of writing.

If I were to paraphrase Alex's theoretical position, based on what he says here, I might do it this way: Writing is a craft, a set of skills that we learn through practice. In a composition course, or a sequence of composition courses, students get that practice. As long as the teacher is willing to be a little flexible, and as long as the students take advantage of the opportunities presented to them, they will learn.

Given the simplicity of Alex's theory and the extent to which it meshes with the theory he sees underlying the text and the program, there is little sense of dissonance in his teaching, and thus apparently little reason to explore theoretical questions. In the course of our conversations, Alex rarely mentions any readings or discussions from the teaching seminar, and never raises those nagging questions about the nature of teaching writing that sometimes torment his peers. It is only later, when he reads an early draft of this chapter, that Alex writes:

> *For me, I guess, I needed to experience teaching myself both as a writer and as a theorist. I wanted to have conclusions before I weighed them against others. That way, I can evaluate and say, "Oh yeah, that's where I messed up." If I didn't do that, I felt, I would be lost in someone else's sense of self.*

From this it seems to me that Alex still sees theory as something outside himself, something that he must "put on" as he would put on a jacket or tie. In fact, he uses just this language when he says he views theory *"as a complement, like a nice tie to a good suit."* Theory, in Alex's view, may *complete* experience, pull it together the way the right tie can pull together the colors in a shirt, jacket, and pants, but it cannot substitute for experience. *"Theory cannot be the suit,"* he writes in the margin of the manuscript. *"If it is, the person beneath is lost."*

### Rhetorician in Training

Like Alex, Keith seems not to have felt serious tensions between the
courses he taught last year and the implicit theories of teaching writing
that he brought with him from undergraduate school. In fact, with his
emphasis on the need for motivation, constant practice, and clear
communication, he sounds very much like Alex:

> See, my attitude about writing is that it's like speaking another
> language, and the best way to improve is to do it, and through
> practice . . . you get better. So I think a good deal of teaching
> writing is motivating students to write. That sounds simplistic,
> I'm sure. And then, in responding [to a business letter], when
> somebody does something that—well, I don't like to use the term
> "wrong" but, for lack of a better term—when [it] seems they're
> [being] too familiar, or being too friendly, I point that out and say
> that in this situation, this part of your style is going to cause a
> problem in communication.

Of all the TAs, Keith is the one who talks about theory most explicitly. Though he sometimes speaks of theory in negative terms, as in his
occasional shots at Derrida and poststructuralist literary theory, he
seems to have a fascination with the *idea* of theory and he is clearly
interested in how and why we teach writing. Still, had he been teaching 101 this semester, Keith might have felt as little need as Alex for a
unifying theory to base his teaching on. It is this new course, "Business
and Technical Writing," that creates the dissonance that lures him into
theoretical waters:

> I wanted to find something that I could tie the whole course
> together with. Tanner [a young linguist in the department] uses
> that theory of communication which is a very complicated prag-
> matic theory I found out. . . . I don't understand it well enough
> myself to explain it clearly to students. But I'm going to use a
> communication theory involving the use of the "you attitude,"
> when we're talking about business letters and memos—writing
> things where you're trying to get a certain response out of people.
> . . . I think I can support about anything using that theory.

Although he sees theory as a practical device, a way of providing
coherence in a course that could be hard to manage, Keith also believes
that theories are useful only if you understand them, and in this
respect he feels a little limited. The linguist's theory, attractive as it is
in many ways, is more sophisticated than Keith is ready for at the
moment, so he pares it down, simplifies it to the "you attitude" concept, which he thinks will serve his purpose. In its reduced form,
Keith's "you attitude" theory—essentially a rhetorical approach based

on appeal to audience—gives him the perspective he needs to envision the course as a whole and thus to launch himself into the semester.

When I ask Keith what he means by the "you attitude," a concept I recognize as a fairly standard staple of business communications textbooks, he says:

> Well, that's just it. I don't understand it that well myself. [Tanner] goes off onto all these overlays, and I wonder how well his students understand it. But it's kind of like the— Well, you know the stress in the [101 textbook] on audience and making the—especially when you're writing a business letter—making the person who's reading that letter think he or she is the most important person in the world, subtly, you know, not like a sweepstakes letter or something. But subtly. And he does that with business letters, memos, résumés, everything.

Although he doesn't use the term "rhetorical," it seems to me that Keith sees the "you attitude" as a basic rhetorical strategy, part of a broader approach which regards writing as geared toward communication and centered in considerations of purpose and audience. For his immediate needs, this approach makes sense to Keith, and it jibes with his layperson's notions of what generally goes wrong in business and technical writing—notions that were reinforced recently when he received a poorly written letter from the university's Office of Continuing Education, thanking him for teaching a summer course at the local Air Force base:

> I thought, "This is great, I can use this, I can find real examples of business letters and memos and résumés that are really obviously done poorly, and we can use those in class and look at those as things to avoid and start from there." So it sort of took some of the pressure off. Rather than me trying to come up with some kind of original theory or borrow someone's theory I didn't completely understand, I was able to get a more practical idea, and when I go home to visit my parents, I'm going to pillage their old files, from different business ventures, and see how much I can bring back.

From the way he talks about theory here, it is clear that Keith has two somewhat different definitions of theory. In the hands of others, people more knowledgeable than he is, theory might be comprehensive, might in fact organize knowledge in broadly systematic ways. This is something he is interested in, something he will later pursue, in fact, when he applies to a graduate program in linguistics at another school, but pragmatically, it's not something he can devote time to now. Now, he must get on with teaching this new course, and for this purpose, a more pragmatic working theory will suffice.

Still, Keith is aware that his "you attitude" approach will take him only so far. In acknowledging that his working theories "sound simplistic," and in commenting repeatedly that he's always learning more that he doesn't know, Keith seems always to be leaving the door open for further reflection, further theorizing.

### Theorizing as a Dialogic Process

Although Keith's attraction to theory at first seems primarily technical, related to his interest in communications, discourse analysis, and linguistics, he also has a philosophical side. That side is very much in evidence late in the semester, when Meredith joins us for a couple of sessions. On one of these occasions, questions about *how* to teach writing give way to questions about *why*, as Meredith's persistent challenges and my nudgings force Keith to consider how he defines good writing and what he sees as the end of teaching.

In one conversation, when I ask Keith and Meredith a question I had asked Mike—whether consensus is desirable or even possible among writing teachers—Keith draws on his weight-training experience to respond:

> You'll have to pardon me for using another lifting analogy, but I always—Every kid I've ever been around who wants to start lifting is always convinced that somewhere out there is somebody who knows the perfect program, that if you only will follow that program, you'll achieve everything you want, get as strong as you want and as big as you want, and that's just not true. But I think writing is similar in that lifting and writing more than anything else require practice, but each individual has a different set of buttons to push.

Soon, the subject turns to what the goal of a writing course should be, and Meredith prods Keith to follow through on his weightlifting analogy: What is the goal of weightlifting? What is the finished product? What does "getting better" mean?

For Keith, these are not easy questions to answer. As in weightlifting, he suggests, the goals of individuals vary. The teacher may be trying to get students to express themselves clearly, but students may be more interested in getting an A in the class.

> The goals, I think, come into conflict. How do you, how do you grade expression? When you read a paper and it's clear and the writing is good, but the real expression underlying it all is [pause] nothing, it's just one of these people who can sit down and there's an A paper.

As he goes on to talk about this particular dilemma, Meredith confronts him with another one: "What's an A paper?"

> *Keith:* I'm not sure [laughs]. I was just thinking, you've got these students whose goal it is to get an A . . . and if you really want them to be thinking deeply about things and expressing themselves honestly, and baring their emotions a little bit, and someone writes a really fine paper as far as mechanics and everything go, but it's got that certain emptiness about it, like "I just did this for the grade, I'm not going to bare my feelings to anyone—"
>
> *Meredith:* It's not necessarily about baring feelings.
>
> *Keith:* Well, I'm not talking about baring feelings in the sense of, "Here I am" [makes an open gesture], but I mean thinking deeply about an issue. So many of the times, some of us would talk about students' reactions, especially in freewriting, to the Gulf War or the [anti-gay] chalking on campus, there wasn't much substance behind what they were saying.
>
> *Meredith:* Then it's not an A paper. You mean that it's written very well in terms of grammar and in terms of—
>
> *Keith:* I'm not saying that it's good writing in general, but for empty writing it's good. [Meredith laughs.] What I'm saying is, how do you get across to these students the difference between what they're writing and writing that goes the next step. How do you teach that?

Here ensues an extended discussion of whether it's possible to call empty writing "good," with Meredith, ever the Socratic questioner, leading Keith into a classic philosophical dilemma:

> *Meredith:* See, I still don't even see that as, I mean, this is what really bugs me because you want to call that good writing, [but] it's not good writing; I mean it's—OK, if it's well constructed and it's—is that what you're trying to say, well-constructed sentences or something?
>
> *Keith:* Well, what I'm saying is, it's a kind of writing that, I mean you're looking for something that you, as hard as you try, it's difficult to put into words, an element of, in the paper, in their expression that is so intangible it's difficult to explain. And they just don't get it but other than that they're, it's a good paper. I mean we can't even put our finger on it.
>
> *Meredith:* You're talking about "voice" maybe.
>
> *Keith:* Well, who knows what I'm talking about [laughs]? I've gotten in over my head; I can see that.

At this point, to use another of Keith's sports metaphors, Meredith has him in deep water. The philosopher in her poses questions that he has no ready answers for, and he feels momentarily out of his depth.

But Keith is not really "in over his head" in this conversation. He just seems to be talking about two things at once: the "utilitarian" goals of his "Business and Technical Writing" class, where "clear expression" means successful communication to an audience, and the more personal goals of a liberal arts education, where "honest expression" means, among other things, willingness to confront emotions. Unlike Meredith, who cannot imagine reconciling these goals, Keith sees nothing contradictory in them. Given what he calls his "diverse" personal background, in fact, they both make perfect sense to him.

### In Praise of Diversity

For Keith, who is discreetly open about being gay, his diverse background comes about largely because of his sexual orientation. As he explains:

> I'm a preacher's kid, and my family is mostly pretty conservative. So I—about a lot of things, I still have pretty straightlaced conservative values, but about other things, obviously [laughs] I don't. And I don't really fit . . . neatly into anybody's slot on the political spectrum.

Because of his conservative background, Keith frequently finds himself challenged by other graduate students, who tend to congregate at the left end of the political spectrum. Although they respect him for his intelligence, thoughtfulness, and humor, they sometimes don't know what to do with this gentle weightlifter who spent two years in the Army, supports the Persian Gulf War, defends Reaganomics, and despises bigotry in any form.

Though occasionally annoyed by his peers' "political correctness," Keith seems for the most part to enjoy disturbing their categories. What they may see as contradictory in his character, he sees as a source of strength. At one point, when I ask him whether he believes teaching is political, he responds:

> Yeah, in the sense that a liberal arts education is supposed to open up new horizons for you and enable you to think critically about diverse issues . . . especially about issues that you don't want to think critically about. [laughs] . . . I think classes are a lot more interesting when you're talking about things that have political or ideological or value basis, something that people are going to feel strongly about. . . . I'm gonna have to keep reminding myself next semester [when I teach 102] not to be getting up on any kind of soapbox no matter what direction discussion takes, because I'd like to introduce different issues and especially bring up how

minority groups view, what their view of America is and American society, what it means to be American.

Because of his dissonant experience, both as a gay male in a homophobic culture, and as a conservative preacher's kid in a liberal academic culture, Keith is especially sensitive to issues of cultural difference:

> It bothers me when, as a student, I express an opinion and other students gang up on me or something . . . When that happens in a class I'm teaching, when someone expresses an opinion, even though I don't agree with them . . . once it starts to seem like a group of people ganging up and attacking, I'll sometimes very subtly almost take the other person's point of view . . . instead of letting them slip into this mob mentality . . . just [to] make it clear that this is simply another way of viewing reality or culture or whatever it is.

Perhaps because he is open to difference, open to cultural diversity, Keith is also open to many theories of teaching writing:

> I think one of the neat things about composition is everybody has so many ideas, and some of them, as far as I'm concerned, are crazy and screwy, but they're all pretty interesting. And I can't remember anybody who had nothing to offer me in terms of some ideas I might try out.

When he leaves the following summer, to begin his linguistics program at another university, Keith will take up a new challenge: teaching minority students in an Educational Opportunities Program. To reach these new students—quite different from the ones he has been teaching at our university—he will need new pedagogical theories, and as he tells me when he comes in to say good-bye, this is a challenge he's looking forward to.

## Return of the Repressed Romantic

At the opposite end of the pedagogical spectrum from Alex and Keith is Peter. Where Alex feels generally comfortable with his teaching, Peter often seems to feel uncomfortable. Where Keith is intrigued by theory in general, Peter seems almost hostile to it. At first, this appears to undercut my own theory that dissonance breeds interest in theoretical questions, but when I look beyond the actual language Keith and Peter use, I see that Peter raises theoretical issues perhaps *more* often than Keith does—he just doesn't see that these are theoretical issues, and that taking an overtly theoretical stance might be the best way of dealing with them.

Coming from an undergraduate background in creative writing and journalism, Peter was one of those in the first-semester practicum who shared Alex's skepticism about composition. But unlike Alex, who seems to have overcome his skepticism and discovered connections between creative writing and composition, Peter still associates composition with the prescriptive pedagogy he always hated. For him, the 101 textbook isn't just a little constraining, it's downright stifling. For instance, he likes the idea of having students read strong model essays—such an approach is consistent with his background in creative writing—but he doesn't really like many of the example essays in the text. Most of all, he dislikes the text's way of abstracting certain "basic features" from those essays and then asking students to include those features in their own essays. For Peter, such an approach smacks of "recipes":

> Deep down inside I think, "Is this really gonna even matter, what I say to them, you know about this unit? Are they getting anything at all from this unit besides reading the short stories [or essays] that are included?" ... Those [models], to me, are, you know, foundations, cornerstones of building on that unit, and the questions that they put after that are very helpful, but this other stuff about, the recipe type stuff—two eggs, half cup of milk, that kind of junk, I'm thinking to myself, "My God," you know, "Am I just deluding myself thinking that they're even gonna learn anything from this?" and I really toil with that, and it really bothers me, because, you know, it's not like math, and it's not like science, where you can spew forth all this stuff. This is a very, very squishy, you-can-shape-it-any-which-way-you-want type of field, and you know, how can you grade different clay sculptures in Play-Doh, you know, when it's out of their minds onto paper, you know, like what they're doing in writing. I really struggle with that.

If he insists that his students write with certain rhetorical features in mind, Peter worries that he will stunt their enthusiasm and creativity:

> If they don't include those [features], I'm wondering if I should penalize them for not including those and kind of going off on their own way, because I don't want to—inside I want to let them spread their wings, and if I feel like I'm closing them down, my worst fear is that I'm gonna shut 'em down even further for the rest of the class and that they're gonna be very timid about the following papers.

When I ask Peter what approach to teaching he might find more appealing, he responds: "That's the hard question, because I don't think you can teach it necessarily in the classroom environment." Probably, he says, the only way to teach writing meaningfully is through conferences. There, the teacher can "help slide somebody in one direction and another, the way a lot of the creative writing teachers do it when they do independent studies." That one-on-one conferencing—" along with the writing groups, I am still a fan of the writing groups"—is the core of Peter's pedagogy. About anything else, he remains profoundly skeptical.

As I listen to Peter offer his views, hesitantly, apologetically, I find myself wishing he had come along twenty years earlier. In the early 1970s, he would have been in his element. Reading Ken Macrorie and Donald Murray, John Schultz and the early Peter Elbow, he might not have felt the alienation he now feels from both his text and his teaching seminar. For Peter, as for those pioneers in composition studies now labeled "romantics" or "expressivists," the real role of the writing teacher is to motivate, to inspire, to help students overcome fears and writing blocks and develop confidence in themselves as writers:

> When they try to do something different instead of staying "normal," they try to go out of the way and do something a little bit more avant-garde or artsy or whatever. It's nice to see them try to spread their wings a little bit. It's one thing to see the little sparrows on the ground just kind of walking around, but when they start flapping and they're still not going but they're at least flapping, it's exciting. And I like to see that.

Although he doesn't feel support for his theories in the textbook or in the teaching seminar, it is not hard to see where Peter's pedagogical ideas come from. Even more than Keith and Alex, Peter bases his implicit theories on his own personal writing background.

## The Call of Stories

Although Peter often refers to the writing he's engaged in now, either for graduate classes or on his own, he doesn't say much about his writing background until I ask him to tell me about it. "I seem to have the best memories from writing creatively," he says. "By that I mean, like, just stories." A couple of those stories have turned up recently, and Peter laughs as he tells me about them, but most of his school writing was not particularly memorable:

> Most of the other stuff, it was kinda old school crap. Single lines, double underlines, "i before e"—all that other grammar crap. So the writing wasn't that much fun. I do remember reading more than anything.

Peter's positive associations with reading stories were formed very early when his mother and elementary school teachers would read stories aloud. Then there was a long gap, in the grammar-intensive junior high years, before writing became "fun" again. In high school, Peter remembers interesting assignments, like

> "Write a report about my favorite rock group and why," and "Dissect the lyrics of a song." And that was a lot of fun. I remember that. That was tenth-grade English.

Later he says,

> It was a lot of fun in high school, because the teachers there were like, "Wow"—it was really good, there was a lot less emphasis on that grammar crap and more on the writing itself, and I think that reflects with my students, too. They really like the story that they wrote [for the first assignment].

Because of the positive associations he has had with story writing, Peter is eager to give his students similar opportunities—opportunities to "spread their wings," take some chances, try "artsy" things with language. For this reason he began the semester with a "creative writing" assignment that seems to have been the highlight of the semester for both him and his students. When I ask him why he thinks that assignment worked so well, he responds with his characteristic jumble of metaphors:

> Well, it could have been just simply because it was the beginning of the school year—they were all excited as puppies at Christmas, you know. But I think that because they kinda had free rein— They've each got this horse, and they can go wherever they want with that horse. So they hop on and they just go. Some of 'em go slow, some of 'em go like a bat outta hell, and they're just real happy about having that freedom. But when you start putting constraints on them for their writing, "OK, you write this paper, it's got to be at least, it should include the following, it should have such and such of a tone." And then it starts whittling down. It seems like it's progressively whittling down on their enthusiasm for the course when you start slapping on a couple of ankle weights, "OK, now, you can only wear a bright red coat when you're out there on the horse, plus the ankle weight, plus you have to have a purple hat—you can't have a black hat, you can't have a white hat—so everybody's gotta wear purple, and make sure that when you go around this tree you go around it from right to left and not from left to right when you come to it." And I say, "When you get to that trough by the creek, you can't take a drink out of it; you can go through it, but you can't stop and take a drink." All these little stupid constraints, not stupid necessarily, but some of them maybe are in their eyes stupid constraints, like

[the 101 textbook] is perhaps trying to give them pointers on what makes a good paper, but maybe some of them, especially some of the more advanced students, might want to say "the hell with it" and go on their own.

The theory that Peter gives for beginning with this "creative" assignment is that it gives the students the freedom they need to develop confidence, overcome their fear of writing before they move on to more "objective" forms. Ironically, though, this theory doesn't seem to have worked with Peter. Although he feels fairly confident about the short stories he's producing for his creative writing workshop, Peter admits he has an "attitude" about critical analysis, and this attitude is causing him problems in graduate school. On the one hand, he's aware of how his experience affects his students: "I don't want what's happening to me to happen to them," he tells me. But on the other hand, he clearly doesn't feel enough confidence in his own academic writing to teach from what he knows. Consequently, he's thrown back on the textbook, whose "recipes" and "constraints" he doesn't believe in.

As I listen to Peter voice his frustrations, I hear him raising serious issues: How important is academic writing? How do we learn it? How do we sequence writing activities in meaningful ways? But when I try to nudge our conversations into more explicitly theoretical territory, asking Peter to expand on his critique of the textbook, or prodding him to recall something we had talked about in the teaching seminar, he doesn't take the cue. It's not as if he's unwilling to theorize about his own experience—in a way, his metaphors are theoretical discourse. It's just that he's not able, or perhaps not ready, to hear the voices of others, and this is something he shares with several of his peers from last year's seminar.

---

I have mentioned before Peter's resistance to the TA seminar texts. Except for Mike Rose, whose style he found engaging, he had little good to say about the seminar readings, most of which he found dull and boring—a far cry from the Raymond Carver stories he preferred to read. And Peter was not alone in this opinion. Among the twelve TAs in the teaching seminar last spring, few seemed to find the theoretical reading engaging. Though their journal entries were usually thoughtful and intelligent, their responses tended to take off on tangents from the readings rather than engage them directly. In fact, as I

said in the preface, I often had the feeling that they were only skim-
ming the texts I assigned, reading just enough to write a journal response and then turning back to what they considered the "real texts"
for the course—their own classrooms, their own students, their own
stories.

Actually, I am fairly sympathetic to such resistance. Most inexperienced TAs feel frustrated and insecure about their teaching—and
about their own graduate work, as well. Their attention during these
first semesters is on immediate matters: how to get students to stop
cutting classes, how to deal with plagiarizers, how to respond to a peer
who criticizes their handling of a situation, how to manage their time.
With these matters and others demanding their immediate attention,
is it any wonder they find their own stories more compelling than
Gere's history of writing groups or Knoblauch and Brannon's discourse on the development of modern rhetoric?

And my sense is that they *do* learn a good deal from their own
stories. For instance, Peter seems to have a reasonable theory about
what made him a writer: listening to his mother read stories as a child,
trying out his own stories, being urged to spread his wings, to take
chances, to write like he talks, to share his writing with peers. He even
seems to be aware of the limitations of his experience, regretting that
his one-semester required undergraduate writing course offered no
exposure to the kind of academic writing he is now being asked to do.
Still, like Keith's "you attitude" theory, Peter's stories can only take
him so far. They don't give him what he seems to need most at this
point in his career: a way of contextualizing his frustrations, understanding them in the light of other stories that both corroborate and
challenge his implicit pedagogical theories.

## Subverting the Text

While Peter only senses that his own theories of writing are at odds
with the course he is teaching, Meredith is sure of it. Still, she is
reluctant to admit this to me. As she says in one of our earliest interviews, "I still have a sense [that] I should censor certain stuff, you
know, before I tell you." Because she is a little more secure in her
teaching than Peter is, however, she soon finds herself telling me about
a letter she has been writing to a friend at another school:

> I said I wanted to throw the textbook away. It says [reading from
> the letter] "I skimmed the comp book yesterday and felt like
> throwing up [laughs]. I just felt like chucking the textbook com-

pletely." Then I wrote: "subvertly." I don't even think that's a word. "I don't even see any reason to pretend that I'm bound by the textbook this semester."

Because she was so unhappy with the designated 101 textbook last year, Meredith opted for an alternative this semester, but she's already unhappy with it: "This is just as bad as [the first text], only there's less of it. So what's the difference?"

As she goes on to talk about this issue, it becomes clear that her dissatisfaction is not just with the text but with the course itself. "What exactly is 101?" she asks. Last year, a student told her it felt like a repeat of high school, and she suspects that the student may be right. When I ask how she might redesign the course if she had the freedom to do so, she has a clearer idea than Peter does of where she would like to take it:

> Well, I was thinking a lot about this reader-response stuff that we did with Phil, and I thought that I learned so much in there, even though I wasn't—I mean some of the stuff we read I wasn't thrilled with, but I think I would set it up that way, where we would just have different sources like film and literature, and [inaudible] where they would just write . . . I think I would set it up like that somehow, where they were doing journals constantly in response to whatever we were reading or seeing or— And then, I don't know, I don't know what— Because now I'm more topic-oriented. I have these, I look at the book chapters and I pick, you know, topics that fit with the book chapters. So I'm more topic-oriented instead of theory-oriented or method-oriented or what-ever . . .

Later, Meredith will recall that her dissatisfaction with these 101 texts parallels her dissatisfaction with some of the readings for the teaching seminar last spring. With some of those authors, she had been so impatient that she simply stopped reading. When she did, she would "confess" to this in her journal, almost daring me to call her on it. In other semesters, as I said in the preface, I probably would have, but because I was burned out myself that semester, I didn't have the energy to deal with such rebellions. And besides, Meredith's provocative discourses on the uselessness of the readings sometimes had as much theoretical content as anything I had assigned the class to read. Impressed with the quality of her thought, I gave in—not realizing until later that though she was stretching *me* in this process, she herself might have profited from some stretching in return.

As for the sources of Meredith's impatience with the readings, I suspect they were multiple. Like Peter, she balked at the language she was reading—though not quite for the same reasons. As Peter himself acknowledged, part of his resistance to academic discourse was due to his inexperience with it. At his undergraduate school, there was only one required composition course, which emphasized personal writing, and after that he spent most of his time in creative writing and journalism classes. With Meredith, an old hand at complex academic discourse, the question was not whether she could read abstract and analytical language but whether the game was worth the candle. She thought it was not.

More important than the language, then, was the content of the readings in the seminar, and this for Meredith was a grave disappointment. To be perfectly honest, I don't think I understood at the time the nature of Meredith's objection to the readings. Though she was quite open about her resistance, it wasn't until I got to know Meredith better, in the course of this project, that I began to understand why her attitude was so strongly negative. It wasn't, as in Peter's case, that the readings didn't offer practical guidance. Nor was it simply that they contradicted her own implicit theories. The problem, I began to see, was that many of those readings didn't even raise the questions that Meredith saw as most important. Instead of focusing on *why* we teach writing, they mostly focused on *how* we teach writing, leaving unanswered—even unaddressed—the questions Meredith always finds more interesting and most important. As she puts it,

> It's not writing, but writing about what—that's the question. . . . I think this is where I have the problem, because I can't teach form. The content always becomes the primary thing somehow. It doesn't make sense to me to talk about teaching somebody a skill, teaching somebody good writing, and then the philosopher in me just [says], "All right, what do you mean by good writing?" And that's why the kids say that English teachers, that English is subjective, because everybody, every teacher has their own ideas about what good writing is.

Meredith herself has strong ideas about what makes good writing. In her view, it isn't technical proficiency, formal coherence, or rhetorical efficacy. Good writing, for Meredith, is writing that leads the students to self-discovery:

> I want them to learn things about themselves, but you don't learn things about yourself in a vacuum. I mean, you have to—you learn things about yourself by the way you respond to the rest of the world.

Because she believes the most worthwhile way of responding to the world is through personal writing, and because she has seen personal writing associated with an "expressivist" point of view, Meredith sometimes uses that term to define herself. At one point, for instance, Meredith describes a telling moment that occurred in class that week when a student responded to a textbook prompt about writing an essay on a remembered person:

> So some guy raised his hand and he said, "I have a question about Number 2—which is, 'Who would be interested in this person and the point you want to make about him or her?'"—and I said, "What's your question?" and he says, "Well, who cares?" [laughs]. I was so—"What do you mean 'Who cares'?" and he says, "Well, what if nobody else is interested, what difference does it make?" And all of a sudden all of that, all of those things that I wrote, you know, in the journal for [the teaching seminar], talking about expressivism versus the rhetoric—[here she stops to search for an opposite to expressivism]—all of a sudden all that stuff came back to me, just rushing back to me [laughing], and it's like it was all just completely congealed into this one thing that this student said: "Well, who cares?"

Clearly, the question of "who cares" is central to Meredith's theory of teaching writing. For her, it seems, writing means exploring identity, exploring values, and ultimately, it need satisfy no one but the writer.

Because Meredith likes to engage in philosophical discussions, and because her strongly held positions tempt me to play devil's advocate, I introduce, in some of our conversations, standard objections to the expressivist point of view. Can teachers fairly grade expressivist writing? Can we recognize when it's "authentic"? Is it fair to the students not to prepare them for the kinds of writing they will need to succeed in college and jobs? For most of these questions, Meredith has thoughtful answers, and throughout our discussions, she defends her approach to teaching—an approach that she sees as dictated by her values and her "worldview." At the end of the course, she will also quote proudly from students' journals and from course evaluations that testify to the effect the course has had for them: "I think the course helped us [learn] how to voice our own opinions," "The instructor inspired me to write my best. She helped me write in a way that I could express myself." For Meredith, these responses are an important validation. She has taught according to her theory, and these are just the results she was hoping for.

## "I Don't Want to Do to My Students . . . "

In some ways Meredith is a lot like Peter—a humanist in the postmodern age—and despite enormous personal differences, I see connections between them. Both see their students primarily as people, with human needs that take precedence over academic needs. If writing is to mean to these students what it means to Meredith and Peter, it must allow them to express their fears and worries, their problems and conflicts, either directly, through journals and personal writing, or indirectly, through stories and responses to books or films.

In Meredith's own life, writing has been "like a bodily function to me . . . like a survival mechanism." As a child, she says, she "wrote all the time," from stories in first grade through school writing that got her "in trouble" because it wasn't what the teacher wanted. Because her school experience, like Peter's, came close to destroying writing for Meredith, she is determined, like him, that she will not do the same thing to her students: "I don't want to do to my students the same thing that was done to me, or that I felt was done to me," she says, echoing his remark.

When I ask Meredith what she means by this, her response recalls what she had said earlier about the question of audience:

> I was just thinking about this. I've been thinking about this a lot, trying to write, messing back and forth with this idea of dissertation and whether I—. . . I'm trying to plan, get the idea in my head of what a dissertation would be. But every time I sit down and try to write a paper about literature, or about what I'm reading, it's back to the way it was when I tried to write for [my other graduate program] or what I tried to write for any class. . . . It's the audience, . . . what is the audience you're writing for? And I feel like I have to write for this abstract . . . academic audience, and I was thinking about that and I thought, "Well, who is that, what is that, it's not anybody, it's not a person, it's just some thing" . . . and I started thinking how ridiculous that was, I mean, it seemed ridiculous to me [laughing] . . . Makes more sense to me to think about, when I'm writing something, writing it to a person or writing it to myself, not writing to this academic thing out here. So that's what, when I'm teaching, that's why I keep having this conflict.

Like Peter, Meredith seems to have "an attitude" about academic writing, an attitude that grows out of personal experience. But whereas Peter's attitude is grounded primarily in his own personal writing experience, Meredith seeks to ground hers in a context of theory—theory that is probably drawn less from composition studies than from the humanistic tradition she is steeped in.

Although I'm aware of many problems with Meredith's critique of academic writing, and although I play devil's advocate with her from time to time, I respect the moral stance that underlies her theories.

Perhaps it is because of Meredith, in fact, and her persuasive defense of "expressivism," that I am tolerant of Peter's admitted "attitude" toward critical analysis. On the other hand, perhaps it is because of Peter, who does not seem to have the critical resources that Meredith does to name and defend his teaching philosophy, that I am still not entirely persuaded by her argument.

## The Illusion of Objectivity

Like Meredith, Mike seems to reflect frequently on what writing is, how we learn it, and why we teach it. In his journals for the seminar, he would often raise these questions, and our discussions of the courses he taught last year are often grounded in theoretical issues. To some extent, as I suggested earlier, I think Mike's theorizing is a function of his reflective personality: he simply *likes* theoretical discussions. But as with Meredith, some of Mike's thinking is prompted by dissonance—the sense of being somehow out of sync with the course he is teaching.

In 101 last year, Mike felt that dissonance early. But he wasn't able to articulate it for himself until late in the semester, when he stumbled onto an insight that had eluded him before. Now, a year later, he explains what happened in this way:

> Something just really clicked over and just made a tremendous amount of sense, personally, as opposed to making sense logically. I dunno if that's a distinction that makes any sense, but I was centering that first course around the [rhetoric text]. I was trying to let the book do the teaching, and I was there to sort of disseminate knowledge, and I didn't feel a lot of connection with the [text]. It's not how I would approach writing. It had some techniques in it which were useful, I think—you know, cuing the reader and talking about counterarguments and so forth—but for the most part I really didn't know what to do with it so I just sorta said, "Here are some examples and let's talk about [them]."

On that particular day, though, Mike was focusing on descriptive language—something he felt comfortable with, having worked on it extensively in creative writing classes. Rather than follow the book, he simply followed his own plan:

> I had people reading in class, breaking up into groups and finding ... what they felt from reading the story, what those emotions were and then what those were tied to, what words were used to do that, whether they thought that worked. And people got really excited about that.

One reason Mike felt good about this class was because it was one of the rare times that semester when he was really comfortable with what he was teaching. Working with other kinds of writing—position papers, for instance—he had felt unsure of himself, alienated by the unfamiliar vocabulary of the text.

> Some of it I understood, but the language was different, you know, counterarguments and so forth. I always thought, "Put yourself in the other guy's shoes"—I didn't call it counterarguments.

As I listen to Mike, I'm not always sure what it is about the text he finds so alienating. Sometimes, as in the above example, it seems to be a matter of language.

> I am not versed in the language and the concepts and the way of thinking about it that these textbooks are, so I'm sort of appropriating that language, 'cause that's what I'm asking them to read, and then I'm trying to make that mesh with what I understand about writing, but it's not a perfect fit because I'm only, I'm only coming across it maybe three or four days ahead of them.

In other situations, though, it seems to be more than the language of the text that Mike is resisting. Sometimes the whole pedagogical approach doesn't jibe with his implicit theories, his sense of how he himself learned to write in undergraduate creative writing classes:

> I guess the persona that I had, the reading persona that I have for my own writing that I've developed from the creative writing stuff as an undergrad is so second nature to me that there's no structure, there's no conscious structure in there. I read through it and I go, "Ah—I'm responding this way to it, I'd better fix that."

At another point, he explains:

> I very rarely think of my writing as process. . . . That's one of my problems that I have with education in general is that it's— Supposedly there's knowledge out here in this area and . . . the way we're going to teach this knowledge is to break it down into these pieces, and here's every part, every point in this process, but that's not how we learned it. We learned it by continuous feedback, by writing and getting response, and writing and getting response and writing and getting response. I think that's why I don't recognize that [textbook] stuff, because I was never taught the process, [and] the times that people tried to teach me process with grammar and with sentence structure and so forth, it just went right over the top of my head.

Hearing Mike use the word "process" in an unexpected way, I ask him what he means by this term:

> Well, I mean like breaking down your writing into minute parts
> . . . I'm not talking about just introduction, body and conclusion;
> I'm talking about breaking your introduction into a topic sentence,
> your thesis statement, like [the text does] with the position paper:
> OK, each paragraph has to have a topic sentence, and then you're
> going to elaborate on that. That's not the way—I mean maybe
> that's the way I write, but that's not the way I've ever thought
> about the way that I write, so it's hard, it was really hard, it was a
> huge, felt like there's just a huge distance between that and what
> I did . . . . I don't know if that reliance on doing it point by point
> produces good writing. I think that produces a reliance on follow-
> ing rules. And I think that I got much better papers; I think that's
> why the remembered events papers were better, because I—at that
> point, it was the last paper in the class and I said, "Forget the
> rules," and we just looked at descriptive language.

In some ways, Mike's rebellion against the 101 textbook surprises me.
For one thing, I had always regarded the text as rhetorical in approach,
rather than rigid and rule-based. Given Mike's background in creative
writing, though, and the "romantic" pedagogy of many writers' workshops, I am not surprised that he finds the text's approach too analytic
for his tastes. What confuses me more is an apparent inconsistency
between what Mike says here, about 101, and what he says elsewhere
in our interviews about the need for "rules and structures" in teaching
writing.

In the course he is teaching this semester—the 200-level "Business
and Technical Writing" course—Mike seems to rely heavily on such
rules and structures. I see this even in our earliest conversations, when
he expresses confidence about teaching the course, citing his experience as a psychology undergraduate, working with style manuals,
APA format, and "various strict rules": "I know a lot more about, or I
feel I know a lot more about 'Business and Technical Writing'," he says.
One thing he likes about the course is that the writing assignments are
easier than 101 papers: "Everything's broken up into nice little sections."

Although I'm curious about this apparent contradiction early in our
interviews, I don't actually ask Mike about it until midsemester, when
he talks about teaching memo format to his students:

> There's a whole structure to it, you know, and they have—I mean
> there's all these rules, and I don't understand the rules. I know the
> principles, the philosophies: "Keep it clear, concise, don't waste
> any words, make sure everybody gets all the information they
> need, make it easy to read." . . . So that's what I'm trying to mesh
> with the language of [assuming the text's voice]: "The format of
> this is Purpose, Summary, Discussion, Action. OK, and you want

> these set off and these are the types of things you put in this
> section and that section."

Surprised that he is so willing to embrace "rules and formats" such as
these that seem to me far more rigid than anything the 101 text pro-
pounded, I ask Mike whether these rules make sense to him.

> Yeah, all the rules feel like rules to me. I mean they feel like
> concrete statements of things that I've understood all along. That's
> the way that I study, you know, that's the way that I learn: it's like,
> I don't have a name for some things, and then I'll read it and I'll
> see that this is [the text author's] language for something that I
> know, and "Oh, OK," and then those two things go together, you
> know. So the rules do feel like, you know, they feel like rules.

From what he says here, it seems as if Mike has nothing against a
rule-based pedagogy—as long as the rules make sense. But this is
where things start to get confusing—because not everybody, says
Mike, needs to know the rules:

> And that's the difference for me between the learning and the
> teaching. Because you don't need to know what the names of
> those things are to do it, you know. . . . A lot of my writing is sort
> of natural, in terms of—it just feels right. That's the way I ap-
> proach grammar, I don't know the names of these things. I don't.
> I'm hard pressed to identify clauses and— But [in] my writing . . .
> I don't have any problems with that. I can tell you whether it's
> right or wrong; I just can't tell you what the name of the rule is for
> it. So if I was teaching a course in grammar, then I would have to
> start putting together what I know about how I write . . . with, you
> know, [with] what they call that.

When I ask Mike why teachers need to know these rules, he replies:

> Well, maybe they don't. But somehow the students need a struc-
> ture for that. . . . See, you can learn it naturally without those rules
> or those labels, but you can't teach it, you know, except by exam-
> ple. . . . But I mean can you imagine trying to teach a course like
> that? "Don't do it this way, do it this way." "Why?" "Well, I dunno,
> doesn't this sound better? I don't like the way that sentence
> sounds; it sounds better to put it this way." And some of those
> rules maybe I could come up with on my own. . . . But some of the
> other stuff, like the structure of, talking about the Purpose, Sum-
> mary, Discussion and Action, I wouldn't have come up with that.

While Mike concedes that he "would not have thought of putting all
of that into the memo, let alone in that order," he says the format, once
he understands it, makes sense to him:

> You know, it doesn't make sense to me in terms of "Oh, yeah,
> that's what I've always done," but it seems logical. I like the

system, I like what it looks like, it's very ordered and even covers everything, and it fits with what I know about—see, it's also in other areas because, you know, my undergrad [major] is in psychology and English, and in psychology I got into education and learning theory, a lot of learning theory, and it, "Business and Technical Writing," especially with memos . . . just fits everything I've ever heard about learning and how you get information. I mean you prime the reader, at the very beginning there's a line that says "subject," and that's maybe three words long, and then your purpose statement is sort of the subject elaborated, and then your summary is a summary of the whole document, so you're just building more and more about what they're—"Here's what you're gonna read about, here's a little more of what you're gonna read about, here's a bigger picture of what you're gonna read about, here's what you're reading about, here's what I want you to do." And it just intuitively makes sense, but not in terms of anything I've ever written, you know.

Here especially Mike seems to contradict what he had said earlier about teaching 101. There, he talked about throwing out the rules, about "making sense personally as opposed to making sense logically." Here, he seems perfectly satisfied with a rule-based approach, accepting the "logic" of the form prescribed by the writing text.

What explains this apparent contradiction? Are the two courses so different that they require completely different approaches? Sometimes, this is what Mike seems to be saying:

With technical writing, the whole point is that it's supposed to, you're supposed to get the point across. . . . I guess I'm just as guilty as the next person; I like the concept of being able to just follow those rules and just get the minimum down, just strip it down to the bare essentials. That sorta feels like behaviorism to me, behavior modification—the same thing that attracted me to that for a while. There's a set of underlying rules that describes behavior and the learning process, and this is how it goes and you can call it whatever you want but it's always this. And this is right and that's wrong; it's very easy to make those calls because your purpose is always the same, to communicate effectively in a short amount of time and not wasting space and no miscommunications. Whereas I guess I see . . . the writing we do in Comp I and Comp II as being more, I don't know, but it's a different kind of writing, and it doesn't make sense that the rules there— The purpose is different.

Still, even for Mike the issue is more complicated than that, for he is tempted to import some of the "structured" approach to teaching 209 into his 101 and 102 classes. Just two weeks earlier, speculating about why peer groups seem to go better in 209 than they did in 101 or 102, Mike had remarked that the standard formats for business and technical writing made it easier for students to critique each other's work. Then he had mused:

> I wonder if you could do that in composition somehow. . . . I bet you could do this with [an argument paper] real easily. Maybe in your rough drafts you could have them, as part of the creation or the brainstorming or the revising process, you could have them make artificial sections and . . . say, "OK, the purpose is this . . . and your subject is such and such, and your arguments are such and such," if you could break those up into areas and then see if all the points, find out what those rules are, I don't even know, exactly; I mean, even as I'm talking about this, I can't, it's not clear to me what those connections between all those areas might be.

Another occasion on which I notice Mike's attraction to the "rules and structures" he says he despises occurs in our very first interview, when he talks about last year's 102 class. One thing he did in that course, he says, was to give his students more control, including free choice on their last writing assignment. When two students proposed to write short stories, Mike was a little uncertain how to handle it, but then he decided to make it a challenge for them:

> I know a little bit about creative writing, too—certainly more than the people who chose to do that—and so I hit 'em with the full—I wanted to show them exactly what that—" This is a valid form of writing and it has it's own rules. Just because it's creative writing doesn't mean you can do anything; you still have to follow certain conventions." So I hit 'em with everything. I didn't hold anything back, but I wasn't there to tear the pieces apart but I just let them know that, "Well, if you're gonna do this, you're gonna hafta— Well, dialogue always has to go this way, you hafta watch out for your tag lines because this gets boring— 'he said, she said'—you don't want to hear that"—all of this other stuff. And I got rewrites out of it, and people, you know, people took it pretty seriously. So I think they learned something about it.

From this conversation and others, it is clear that Mike is not as averse to "rules and structures" as he sometimes seems to be. But that doesn't mean he's guilty of muddled thinking. What seems to Mike unnatural from the writer's point of view ("That's not the way I write.") is attractive from the teacher's point of view for practical reasons. Sometimes, as in 209, it helps him explain a kind of writing he has little experience with. Or it helps him solve practical problems, like how to respond to student papers and guide peer-group critiques. With "rules and formats," there is something concrete to look for in a piece of writing: either it follows the rules and conventions or it doesn't; either it includes the required material or it's not complete.

Still, this approach may be less than satisfying for Mike in the long run. Like the elaborate point system he has devised for calculating grades this semester, his attraction to rule-based pedagogy may be motivated by a futile desire to maintain "objectivity." As he says about that system:

> I guess I'm sort of exploring this issue of can you remove the personal element, in a way, or something like that. You know what I mean, though? Making it, removing myself from position of judger, you know, sort of saying—it's false, it's really artificial, I think— "Well, these are the standards, and this is what the institution says, and this is what the book says, and so forth, and what you write matches up to that, and I just judge that, it's not my fault if—" You know what I mean?

In recognizing the "falseness" and "artificiality" of his attraction to objective methods of evaluation, it seems to me that Mike is well on the way to sensing a similar "falseness" in the rules and formats approach that he has taken to teaching "Business and Technical Writing." If he has found no compelling need yet to question that approach, it may be, as he says, because his primary need is simply to get through the course this first time, to survive it. Once that dissonance is resolved, once he knows that he can teach "Business and Technical Writing," he may be ready to confront this other dissonance: the contradictions in his own implicit theories of teaching.

## A Dissonance Within

My sense that Mike is torn between conflicting theories—that the dissonance he feels is as much within him as without—is most apparent when he talks about teaching 102 last year. In that course, much more than in 101 or 209, he was able to hit his stride, to come out of the shadow of the text and teach from his own authority. As he explains it:

> That whole second semester was basically playing it by ear. We used the book for some things, and sometimes the students would come up with an idea and we'd use that, outside sources and things for papers, and it was real—I don't wanna say out of control; it wasn't chaotic or anything—but it wasn't following any definite structure other than, "We're gonna learn how to write from different sources." That's the only thing I took into that semester was, "Well, sources are everything," so I was prepared for them to come up with sources that I wouldn't have thought of,

and we spent a lot of time talking about what a source was and
whether you could rely on them or not and so forth.

Because he could draw on his experience coming out of 101, and
because he didn't feel so constrained by the text in 102, Mike was able
to relax and enjoy his 102 class. He was also able to draw on and
develop more fully his own implicit theories of writing and teaching—
theories that differ dramatically from the "behaviorist" pedagogy he
espouses in 209.

Here, for instance, is a long segment from one of our midsemester
interviews. Mike has just received the department memo asking TAs
what they want to teach in the spring, and already he's thinking about
teaching 102 again. What he wants to do this time, he says, is organize
his course around a "culture shock/media" theme:

> At least in the beginning I want to talk about advertising, and the
> media, and the media's presentation of culture, and individuals'
> reaction to that, and see what kind of writing comes out of that,
> 'cause we started, we touched the surface of that I think in 102 last
> time and that was kind of interesting, and it's becoming a little
> more clear to me what was happening there and what else we
> could do.

As he goes on to talk about the course he is imagining, Mike begins to
wax theoretical. He talks about focusing on "analytical reading skills"
and "the way language works," and he begins to wonder whether
these skills might be pursued in 101 as well as 102:

> I don't know if I would do that exactly with 101, but on the other
> hand, why couldn't you? What's really the difference? I mean this
> sounds like a parent saying, "Oh, my child is not old enough to do
> such and such." Why? Who says? . . . I mean it seems, intuitively
> it seems to me that you can do the same things.

Eventually, his thoughts lead him into even broader areas of thought:

> I think education is really kind of a messy hit or miss thing. . . . I
> don't think people shouldn't *think* about it, or try and understand
> what it is that's being accomplished, but at the same time, I'm not
> gonna get too concerned about not knowing every aspect [of]
> where it's going and what it's accomplishing. There's a sense I
> have in composition, in 101 and 102, that something is happening,
> that something good is happening inside that I'm not necessarily
> seeing in their writing, but that it is—if nothing else, there's some-
> thing that's happening in there that's supposedly what's sup-
> posed to happen when you go to college: Your horizons are
> broadened. What other clichés can we throw in? You, something
> happens, you look, you begin to get different perspectives, you get
> different ways of looking at things, and part of that happens in

composition. That's a good forum for me to work with that anyway. For me, it's language and . . . that's the avenue I'm talking about: how to read, and how to think about language . . . to stop taking language for granted. That's exciting to me and I think that does something about the way you approach the world, and it's interesting and I think it's useful and it may not have a directly translatable analog, it may not be anything, say, "OK, now I've taken this, and now I can do such and such."

As he talks about his philosophy of teaching writing—a philosophy as broad in scope as Meredith's—Mike seems to sense that he's contradicting things he's said about teaching 209. Again, he tries to make a distinction:

> I think of composition as—boy this is weird, I wouldn't have said this a year ago—but I think of composition as a creative environment, a creative course that doesn't necessarily have a direct end result, and I think of 209 as a technical course, as "This is just about skills," okay, and that's [how] I set it up in the beginning; I talked about what communication is and so forth and so on. And there are different principles. . . . In composition I'm not applying that stuff from [his undergraduate communications course]—I'm not applying that stuff from that course to composition, or at least not as much, maybe every once in a while, but not as much. There's no room for reader response in 209. Well . . . yeah there is, but not the same way. Do you know what I mean? I mean . . . 209 is strictly about a set of principles that, that work, and either you can follow them or you can't, and composition is a lot more ambiguous to me than that.

Although Mike tries to make a firm distinction here between "Business and Technical Writing" and composition, I can't help noticing the equivocation, the moment when he interrupts himself to admit that there is room for "reader response" in 209. Although he doesn't elaborate on what he means here, I suspect he is talking about "the personal." For in Mike's epistemology, as in Meredith's, the personal plays a very large part.

Over and over in our interviews, Mike talks about understanding things *personally*, about making *personal* connections with his teaching, about the students' *personal* investment in learning. For him, this seems to be where meaning resides: in the personal connection between self and world. When he talks about his struggle with the 101 text, it is in terms of "making the structure personally meaningful, and then teaching from myself, with the structure to lean on and to fall back on." Last year in 102, he says,

> I wanted them to go away somehow, go away from the class with at least the inkling that writing doesn't necessarily have to be a

chore that's assigned in a class that you don't feel any personal connection with. So that's what I wanted them to do is find some kind of personal thing that they were interested in and have them write about that so they can feel what it's like to be interested in what they're doing as they're writing.

And even at the beginning of this semester, as he planned his "Business and Technical Writing" class, he was imagining ways to make the course "personally meaningful" to students. One assignment he had borrowed from his undergraduate psychology professor:

> He sent us out to find publications, professional publications, APA or anything in the field and find some bit of research, and . . . read it, interpret it, and present it to the class and answer any questions the class would have. And I thought it would be really—I'm gonna try and do that for these people. . . . And I just thought that was a really good thing when I went through that because it makes you think differently about yourself and what you're doing in college, when suddenly you're being asked to look at something in your field and really to be a part of that field, to acknowledge that you, you know, "I am part of this field and I understand this stuff, and this is what it is for and this is what I'll be doing," you know. And when you're—when we were made personally responsible for that stuff I felt much closer connection to, you know, the possibility of actually becoming a psychologist was a lot more real to me than it had been just by taking classes and requirements and so forth.

At the time, Mike says he's "excited" about this assignment, and it's true—he's virtually bubbling with ideas. By midterm, though, the excitement has vanished and Mike is teaching more or less "by the book." Why did he let this happen, I wonder? Is it just because the course is new to him? Perhaps. But it seems to me that, in some sense, Mike may always have to struggle against the text—to resist the rules, the order, the authority that hold such attraction for him.

## Conclusion

When I consider the cases of Mike, Keith, and Meredith, as opposed to those of Peter and Alex, it occurs to me that there are certain conditions that create a favorable climate for thinking theoretically. One of those conditions is clearly dissonance—the sense that our implicit theories about what writing is, or how we learn it, or how we teach it, conflict with the theories we encounter explicitly or implicitly in course texts, the program philosophy, or the teaching seminar. When that dissonance is minimal—as it appears to be with Alex, and to some extent with Keith—there is little incentive to think about the values and assumptions that underlie the courses we teach.

Another condition that stimulates theoretical thinking is the presence of a dialogic Other—an Other that may be internally configured, as is the skeptical inner voice Mike continually meets in his reflective discourse, or one that is embodied in a peer or mentor, as Keith's Other is embodied in Meredith and her Other is embodied in me.

The notion that some teachers are more attuned than others to hearing those dialogic Others suggests one other condition that enables a theorizing frame of mind: one must be fairly comfortable in the realm of academic discourse. For Peter, this can be a problem. In resisting the language of academic discourse, he risks shutting himself off from the opposing voices that might make him reconsider and defend his implicit theories. Alex risks some of this, too—though there are signs that he is already overcoming his resistance. When he tells me, in our very last interview, that he hears himself using language he would not have used last year at this time, I am pleased to hear it—not because I am eager that he adopt the jargon of our profession, but rather because I think he may find, as Ann Berthoff argues, that finding names for what we believe and think starts us thinking about our thinking, and that thinking about our thinking inevitably leads us to raise the questions we must raise to keep learning.

This is not to say, I hasten to reiterate, that theorizing can only be done in the language of academic discourse. After all, little of the theorizing of Keith, Mike, and Meredith is conducted in those terms. But the fact is, most experienced college writing teachers live in academic discourse communities, and that is where many of our most stimulating theoretical conversations take place. Although we needn't all speak the language of academic discourse, it is important that we all understand it—if for no other reason than to resist its exclusionary tendencies.

# Interchapter:
# The Theorist in Me

At some point during the course of this project—I don't even remember when—I sat down at the computer and typed out a six-page rant about "theory." I'm not sure what prompted it. A conversation with a colleague? Impatience with an article I was reading? It doesn't matter. I've been struggling with theory, with the *idea* of theory, for a long time, and what boiled over at that point had been simmering on the back burner since—well, probably since graduate school.

It was there, in graduate school, that I first encountered theory, first learned a name for the New Critical literary values I had absorbed as an undergraduate English major. At the time, we didn't call it "theory," though—we were still calling it criticism, as in the "Practical Criticism" course I took my first semester in graduate school. Even there I seem to have had trouble with the idea of theory. When asked to write an essay defining my own theory of criticism, I balked at the task. While my colleagues grew rapturous about Freudian or Jungian approaches (in that course, poststructuralist theory had yet to make an appearance—and even structuralists were represented only by Northrop Frye), I dug in my heels and refused to pledge allegiance to anyone.

Part of my resistance, I'm sure, was simply fearfulness. This stuff we were reading was strange and new, and it undermined what little confidence I had in myself as a serious student of literature. But part of it was something else, as well, and it has stuck with me throughout my career. In many ways, I hear myself echoed in Keith's remarks about theory. On the one hand, I'm attracted to it (like a moth to a flame, it seems). In other ways, I'm repulsed: Is it really necessary to talk about theory in such opaque and abstract language? And why must we limit ourselves to *a* theory, anyway? Like Keith, I seem to be more comfortable with the plural of that word—and with versions of theory I naïvely call common sense and instinct.

When I made the shift, after graduate school, from twentieth-century literature to composition studies, I did so thinking I had somehow escaped to firmer ground. I'm a practical person, it seems, a person who enjoys the challenges of the here and now, and once I got over the initial terrors of teaching writing, I began to develop a deep and abiding appreciation of its complexity. Like a Wallace Stevens poem, a

Virginia Woolf novel, teaching writing is something that grows richer and more various with each experience. I liked teaching writing. I felt grounded there, and from the perspective of a writing teacher, I could even begin to listen in, once again, on those theoretical conversations I had found so alienating in graduate school.

It was never easy. The theoretical readings in Ross Winterowd's NEH Summer Seminar on "Literature and Literacy" at USC in 1982 nearly drove me mad, but they gave me a new perspective on teaching. And in the years since then, I have had numerous occasions to go off on rants against cognitive process theory, poststructuralist theory, feminist theory, social-constructivist theory, Marxist cultural theory, etc. Often, when I'm ranting, a little part of my consciousness steps aside, like the Woody Allen character in *Play It Again, Sam*, and raises an eyebrow at the ranting self: "Feeling insecure today, are we? Feeling a little threatened, perhaps?" But then I find myself wondering: Does Jacques Derrida ever have such a moment? Does Paulo Freire ever look in the mirror and ask: "Taking ourselves a bit seriously today, are we? Sounding a little pretentious?"

In the course of this project, I've tried to come to terms with theory—to understand my resistance to it, and at the same time to acknowledge its inevitable presence in my life as teacher and researcher. Finally I have determined that what I resist is not theory but Theory—not theoretical thinking but theoretical language—and the conventions of academic discourse that dictate the dropping of names at crucial points in the conversation. While writing this very essay, in fact, I debated the wisdom of dropping the names of Derrida and Freire. The fact is, I've been far less influenced by them than by colleagues who have read them. But would readers respond if I mentioned only the names of those colleagues?

In this book, readers will find few formal citations—and yet they will hear throughout the considerable influence of all those theorists whose work has shaped, and continues to shape, my thinking about teaching writing. Some will think I ought to have cited them, ought to have been somehow more "scholarly" in my approach. To these, I can only respond that I have taken quite seriously what I have learned from some of these theorists: that the idea of "authorship" is problematic indeed; that language itself is inherently dialogic, shot through with voices of all those we have read and met and spoken with and listened to; that all our theories are socially constructed, sometimes of the most unlikely and incongruous materials; and that the stories we tell about teaching are really theories in themselves.

And besides, the simple truth is that I couldn't begin to name all the sources of my own theoretical thinking. This is a book about how we learn to teach writing, and it is inevitably influenced by everything I've ever heard or experienced or read. If forced, of course, I could cite the most immediate influences: Peter Elbow, Wendy Bishop, and Donald Schon, whose work I read before I started this project; Deborah Britzman, Nancy Miller, Lad Tobin, and Nancy Sommers, whom I read while the writing was in progress. You may not find all these writers cited in this study, but I think they are present here. In fact, I suspect I could trace the presence here of *every* author I've read over the past twelve months, from Robert Brooke to Susan Griffin, from Elizabeth Minnich to Robert Coles.

But my most important sources wouldn't show up in a bibliography. They aren't published scholars, so you wouldn't know their work as I do. Their names are Keith and Meredith and Peter and Alex and Mike.

# 3 Seeing Yourself as a Teacher

It is May, now, and I am nearing the final stages of my leave project. All through the spring, I have been reviewing transcripts, listening again to my conversations with the five TAs. In the beginning, I had hoped this would be a collaborative venture. I envisioned all six of us awash in transcripts, comparing our conversations, looking for patterns and contradictions. As it turns out, though, only I have time to sort through all the transcripts. The TAs, still immersed in their teacher and student roles, are busy writing theses, planning weddings, looking for summer work. Although they manage to find time to read through their own individual transcripts, only two—Mike and Peter—take the option of earning independent research credit by writing about what they see there.

For Mike, the writing becomes an opportunity to reflect on a recurring pattern he has found in his teaching. The essay he gives me has no title, but it begins with this dream-like passage:

> I remember staring blankly at the board, trying to figure out what the teacher was trying to say. The chalk had paused, briefly silent, and in that silence I had come to the realization that I had no idea what was going on.
>
> They say that sometimes people forget to breathe while sleeping, or that their brains forget to send the signal to keep the heart beating, and they die. This was such a feeling—that the part of my brain which organized the cues around me into my "reality" had ceased to function. I was completely dissociated from my body.
>
> In the past I could have taken refuge in anonymity, retreated within the sanctity of student-ness and shrunk back into the crowd of lecturees. But that "out" was now denied me because I was standing at the board, in front of the class, staring at the chalk in my hand. My hand, my chalk, my lecture, and my problem. I was supposed to be the teacher.

Who is this teacher Mike thinks he's "supposed to be"? Is it the same teacher Meredith and Peter and Keith and Alex see in their minds? Not all of the TAs find it as difficult as Mike does to see themselves as teachers, yet when I review the transcripts of our conversations, I am struck by how often, and in what various fashions, I find them disavowing the teacher role. What does this mean, I wonder.

Is it just a measure of their insecurities, a phase new teachers go through? That's what I assumed when I started. But the more I listen to the new TAs, the more I recognize doubts and denials I still feel after sixteen years of teaching. And I know I am not alone. Research has indicated that some of the most well-established women in academe suffer from what is sometimes called "imposter syndrome"—the belief that they do not belong in the profession, that they have gotten where they are by a mere fluke and will one day be "found out"—and though they may admit it less often, I know many male teachers experience such feelings, as well.

What is it we share, those of us who have trouble seeing ourselves as teachers? Is our reluctance in any way related to our ambivalence about personal/professional boundaries? Does it grow out of some dissonance between our own implicit pedagogical theories and the ones we encounter at the university? As I consider the five TAs in my study, I begin to sketch answers to these questions, begin to see how we conspire with our culture to construct for ourselves as writing teachers the most complex and contradictory roles.

## Teaching as a Process

Of the five TAs in my study, it is Alex, not surprisingly, who seems most comfortable in the role of teacher. At one point, having noticed that he seems to struggle with the role less than the others, I decide to ask him about it directly:

> *Libby:* The role of teacher feels easy for you—I mean, feels comfortable for you.
>
> *Alex:* Easier. Yeah, a lot more this year than last year. Even in the 102 it's a lot more relaxed. I don't think I'm pushing nearly as much this time as I did last time.
>
> *Libby:* Pushing?
>
> *Alex:* Myself. That whole idea of the person who gives wisdom. And I've been trying to encourage the students to take a more active role in things. When discussion's going, instead of asking the question and then answering it, I just ask the question and if no one answers, I just call on someone to answer and then that usually gets things going.

Although Alex is willing to speculate a little about what's "different" in his teaching this year—he's no longer trying to play the role of "the person who gives wisdom"—he is clearly not eager to dwell very long on the subject: "Don't want to think about it too much," he says, laughing. "Bottle it, we'll sell it, we'll sell it."

As I struggle again with my ambivalent reaction to Alex—a reaction that includes both admiration and skepticism—it occurs to me that what may account for the ease with which Alex sees himself as a teacher is the fact that he doesn't expect as much from himself in the beginning. And this line of thought leads me to an idea I have toyed with before: that there is some kind of correlation between the way these young TAs view teaching and the way they view writing.

I wouldn't want to push this idea too hard. Looking for correlations like this might tempt me to force the issue. But when I juxtapose some of Alex's comments about teaching with his comments on writing, I can't help noticing a certain similarity. Here, for instance, is a passage I quoted earlier in which Alex talks about how he explains to his students the need for two composition courses:

> Because it's a process. I tell 'em about my experience, creative writing-wise, that even though I have had years, five and six years of writing workshops, I'm still learning, and I had my composition way back as a freshman undergrad, too, and it's just, it's the repetition. The more you write, the more you recognize your mistakes, and the more you learn how to correct them at the creation stage.

And here is another passage, in which he talks about teaching:

> Teaching is an evolutionary process: you never stop learning. I mean once you do, you stagnate; that's it. Then it becomes tedious, then it becomes work. So long as you can keep doing new things, trying things, and improving.

Just as learning to write and learning to teach are both processes for Alex, they both seem to involve a linear-stage progression. In writing, he tells his students,

> You need that beginning, you need to start off slow, and work your way and get comfortable and then move up to the next stage. . . . The more you write, the more you recognize different stages.

In teaching, too, Alex believes in starting off slowly and moving one step at a time. The first thing he had to learn, he says, was "relating to the students and getting them to talk." "That's been pretty good," he tells me. "I've been pretty lucky with that." After the relationship gets established, there's time to work on other things like getting organized and adapting assignments to students—two things he plans to devote more attention to next year:

> At first, the first fall semester when you teach that first section, it's just something out of the book to do. And even in the spring one, you're varying the assignments but it's still something to do. Now with 101 this last fall, you're varying the assignment, but there's reasons behind it, there's more reasons behind it. You want, OK, I want my student to get this out of it. I want my student to try to learn this skill by writing this paper. It's just a refinement of that idea, which I've been [laughs], I've been hopefully working on, making it reasonable for them to do it.

As these passages indicate, Alex seems to see teaching, like writing, as a linear process—a process in which you can't "leap into one area and try to do it all at once or you'll be overwhelmed." Instead, you need to "master that one area and get confident with it, then you can work on the others." Later, I suspect, he will revise this working theory, discover, as those more experienced have, the recursive nature of the teaching process. After a while he may even begin to question, as have recent composition theorists, the meaning of the process metaphor. In the meantime, though, his metaphor seems to have carried him, as it has carried many a blocked or frustrated writer, through the difficult initial phases of his project: learning to see himself as a teacher of writing.

### Conflicting Images

At the opposite end of the spectrum from Alex is Peter. Much more open about his feelings than Alex, Peter also has the hardest time seeing himself as a teacher. There may be a number of reasons for this, as I've hinted in previous chapters. For one thing, Peter is more self-conscious than the others—"hypersensitive" as he puts it, to what peers and students might think or say of him. For another, Peter still sees himself as very much the student. In our interviews, he is far more likely than are the other four TAs to refer to his own student status. In this respect, his image of being caught in the doorway of a faculty meeting, hearing students outside "running in the halls," is a telling one. But perhaps the most significant impediments to Peter's seeing himself as a teacher are the images of the teacher that he carries around inside his head. In Peter's case, those images loom very large, indeed.

My first glimpse of the teachers in Peter's head comes very early in our project. It is the day before classes begin in the fall, and Peter is talking about his own first-year college experience:

> At [my undergraduate school] it's hard for me to even remember 101, but it was, it didn't seem like the 101 that I ended up teaching.

The 101 down there was taught by a professional teacher who is now getting her Ph.D. here . . . I saw her in the library this summer, had a nice chat with her. She was just very cheerful, and she was firm but she was very cheerful, had a nice attitude about the class, and it was a pleasure to listen to her. And I was trying to emulate all these teachers that I had in the past, and gosh, the only one that came out seemed to be Zeke from seventh grade, and he was an awful teacher, and I dunno why he was the one who popped up out of all these wonderful teachers I had in the past, but I think it was because I was so nervous and afraid. And I think Zeke was very nervous and afraid too, because the teachers didn't respect him, they'd call him Zeke behind his back, 'cause that was his nickname when he was in college or something . . . but anyway, I ended up being kind of very authoritarian and like, "Teacher, leave them kids alone!" The exact opposite of what I wanted to be, I ended up being.

From this anecdote, I can see immediately that the teacher in Peter's mind is a Jekyll and Hyde figure—one side the warm, caring nurturer, cheerful, yet firm; the other the authoritarian monster, object of ridicule, fear, and adolescent rebellion. Both are teachers Peter has known in his years as a student, and both are teachers he's capable of being. Yet despite his best efforts to emulate the nurturing teacher, it's the authoritarian, much to Peter's dismay, who keeps threatening to emerge in his teaching.

Peter's authoritarian side is most evident when he talks about his struggle to control it. Last year, there was an incident when he lost his temper with a student, and he is determined not to do that again. Still, as is apparent in interviews quoted earlier, Peter does have trouble controlling his anger and irritation with students. It may be tempting to attribute his problems to hypersensitivity on his part—as Peter himself does, and as I have done, too, to a certain extent. But the fact is, I can easily empathize with what Peter is feeling, and I have heard that same voice of repressed anger and self-blame in many teachers, both new and experienced. So I suspect there is something more going on here than the merely personal. Perhaps part of the problem may lie in the way we construct the role of teacher—or more precisely, in the way the role of teacher has been constructed for us by the culture and the media.

## "To Touch a Life . . . "

Not long ago, in the window of a kitchen store, I saw a coffee mug which read, "To Teach Is To Touch a Life—Forever." Immediately I recognized the image of the teacher inscribed there. It is the same image Peter invokes in our very first interview:

> I would like to be looked at as a positive influence in somebody's life. Kinda like surrogate kids in a way. I've got a roomful of twenty-two surrogate children. And I want them all to do well. OK, now go out in the world and do well.

The fact that Peter thinks of the teacher as a surrogate parent is interesting, given that his mother, a retired elementary school teacher and librarian, has been a role model for him:

> Granted, it's different completely—she was teaching elementary—but still those kids look at her fondly when she bumps into them. Some of them are professionals doing whatever, and they see her and they say hello and always seem to be very happy to see her. And I would like that about me.

In a previous chapter, I speculated that patterns learned in the family may influence the way we as teachers relate to our students, and Peter may be further evidence of this. But as the coffee mug in the store window testifies, the image of teacher as caring nurturer is not something Peter has learned only at home. That image lies deep in the culture.

Though he doesn't mention the parenting role explicitly after that first interview, Peter's characterization of other positive role models often includes an element of nurturing. In addition to the English 101 teacher mentioned earlier in this chapter, there is the sociology professor who spotted signs of depression and got Peter to see a college counselor just by writing a note in the margin of his failing exam. And even this year, when Peter was struggling with his own writing in a graduate course, his film teacher took the time to sit down with him and show him what he could do to improve his analytical essay.

Whether advising students on personal problems or taking the time to work with them outside of class, this teacher in Peter's head is someone who cares deeply about students. And in his own classes, Peter prides himself on fulfilling that role—never hesitating to reach out to students, to try to "touch the life" of anyone who is struggling or in trouble. Not surprisingly, then, where Peter feels most engaged as a teacher—most useful to his students and most comfortable with himself—is in the conference setting. There he can be himself, get down to "nuts and bolts," and do the one-on-one work he believes his students need.

Unfortunately, the students don't always play their expected roles in this little drama. Instead of responding with gratitude to Peter's offers of help, they sometimes take advantage of his good will, or else they fail to return his effort with hard work of their own. When that happens, Peter finds it difficult to stay in role. Even in conferences, moments of anger and frustration intervene:

> I give them a lot of my time when it comes to reading their drafts. I also give them a lot of my time on their journals, and I give them a lot of time in conference settings. I tell them to call me if they have trouble and some of them do. . . . But I do know that it seems that it's a little bit draining on my part as a teacher, with forty-one students, and maybe because I'm putting so much time into that, I expect them to put as much time in it in return. . . . It bugs me when I feel like I'm tossed in the back seat in lieu of biology.

Later, when he writes about this year's experience, Peter will attribute his frustration to his own personal problems:

> *Some problems were only personal and had nothing to do with teaching. And some problems that had their origin in the professional were compounded by an endless and severe introspection on my part, causing me not to be able to see the positive aspects of my teaching. Because I was over-identifying myself in the role of teacher (as opposed to also acknowledging my role as student), my life tended to fly proudly or lie limp, depending on whether or not I was satisfied with my performance in front of the classes that day.*

## Audience Awareness

One thing that interests me in the passage just quoted is Peter's use of the word "performance." As I get to know Peter over the course of the semester, I realize that he often feels performance anxiety—a result, perhaps, of his perception that he is performing for many different audiences. In addition to his students, who constitute his most immediate audience, he plays to his family, his girlfriend, his peers, his graduate instructors, his teaching supervisor, and to me, in my role as researcher. With all these audiences, Peter is under pressure to prove something: that he is a responsible adult, an attractive man, an intelligent reader, a creative writer, a competent professional, an interesting research subject. That he feels he is performing for me, even as we talk, is evident in his occasional comments about hoping I'm finding useful things in our interviews and feeling sorry that I have to transcribe his rambling monologues. As a student, he feels considerable pressure to perform as well, and it comes from many directions. When he finishes a story for his creative writing workshop, he says, "It was a very good day because finally I've written something that Max [the professor] seems to be very supportive of. On the other hand Brad [his fellow TA] has read it, and he didn't like it very much at all."

As a teacher, Peter performs for both supervisors and students. In one of our sessions, he describes the anxiety he felt when, toward the end of a long day of student conferences, the department chair happened into his office—a large room he shares with several other TAs—to look for something in the storage closet:

> This [student] came in for a second conference—it lasted like half an hour long, and right before we started, Marcia [the English department chair] walks into the office, Merrifield 7, and opens the closet and starts shuffling through boxes of stuff, and she says, "I hope I'm not interrupting anything." "Oh, no, of course not." In the meantime, I've got like these red alert Star Trek things going off in me, deflector shields up, because I'm afraid of saying one thing that's gonna sound like, she's gonna just look at me and go, "What the hell are you talking about" you know [laughing]. I just had this image in my mind that she was gonna be listening in, going, "This guy is really retarded as a TA," and it was just making me more and more flustered having her in there, and she probably wasn't even listening . . . but I'm like making this into this great stage production about how I'm gonna get bounced from the program because I say gibberish while the chair's in my office.

With his students, Peter feels special pressure to perform, partly because he carries with him the popular image of the teacher as entertainer. At midterm, worried that his class is losing momentum with a particular assignment, he evokes the image of the teacher played by Robin Williams in *Dead Poets Society:*

> Maybe I should try to forge my own trail, dammit! [laughs] 'Cause it worked that way with the first paper, got a lot more positive response to that, 'cause—had nothing to do with the [text], I just chucked that, did my old Robin Williams bit, "Rip out that first section!" No, I didn't do that, but I just had nothing to do with the book, and I just told 'em, "Alright, do this, do that," and they wrote it and they really liked it.

This image of teacher as performer is one he's seen embodied in his favorite undergraduate English teacher as well. Throughout the semester, Peter mentions a number of teachers he thinks of as role models in some respect, but it is this teacher, Larry Britt, who comes up most often. I count five separate references to him in our interview transcripts, and each time it seems to be the classroom persona that Peter admires. "Yeah," he says at one point, "the only teacher I can think of who really dented me as far as keeping the class interested was Larry Britt at [my undergraduate school], because I've had him for three or four classes." Later, talking about the relative size of composition and literature classes, Peter remarks, "I remember having mythology with Larry Britt and having sixty people crammed into a classroom that could accommodate thirty-five." Because Britt was such a popular teacher, his classes were always full. In fact, he had so much "verve and excitement about teaching" that he even "made Milton exciting; I don't know how he did it, but he had a high attendance in that class, and everybody learned something in that class."

In some respects Peter would like to emulate Larry Britt: "If I could even tap 10 percent of that [verve and excitement]," he says, "I might be a good teacher as well." And yet he also has some reservations about the efficacy of this particular teaching persona. In the interview quoted above, where he first mentions Britt, Peter goes on to say:

> So he just—sometimes he's a little too excited, and he just rapid-fires stuff out to you like a Gatling gun. Mythology especially was really difficult because he just kept laying this stuff on us.

When Peter himself takes on the teacher's stage persona, what emerges is not so much an impressive performer as a clown or stand-up comedian:

> I think it's kind of an interest thing: I'm trying to retain their interest, and by doing that I tell these jokes, and they're, half the time they're flying over their heads anyway 'cause the humor is so dry sometimes. . . . But with the class I'm just trying to make sure, I hear 'em laugh or something out there and I know that they're awake, you know. It's kinda like if they're not laughing or whatever, then they must not be paying attention.

From the way Peter talks about his performer role here, it's apparent that he doesn't find it entirely satisfying. He doesn't mind "playing the clown" now and then—in fact, he clearly enjoys it—but like anyone, he wants an appreciative audience. If Larry Britt is Laurence Olivier playing to a packed house of London theatre-goers, Peter often feels more like the struggling comedian trying out his routine in a seedy cocktail lounge full of apathetic traveling sales reps:

> Up in front of the class it's like Howdy Doody time, and there I go, because I'm trying to keep these cretins from falling asleep in front of me—no, I don't mean to call them cretins, but sometimes at 8:00 in the morning it's like, "Why did I get out of bed for you?" You know, one of those things.

In more reflective moments, Peter seems embarrassed by his anger at his students. He longs to give up the performer role, to trade it in for something more "serious," but the nurturing role he might adopt in its place is not always accessible to him. For one thing, it's just not practical. After all, he's teaching two classes of twenty-two students each, doing his own academic work, and trying to maintain some modicum of a personal life at the same time. But perhaps even more importantly, the nurturing role somehow fails to acknowledge all the realities of teaching. To teach is not just "to touch a life." Teaching also means dealing with students who don't want to be there, and doing it every day, despite the demands of one's own academic and emotional life. In this respect, says Peter, using another of his telling metaphors, being a TA is like "doing three different concerts at once, shuttling between the stages."

Caught up in the demands of the conflicting teacher roles available to him, Peter finds himself in a classic dilemma—classic because, in one sense, it mirrors the struggles of men and women negotiating gender roles. How can he be both performer and caring nurturer? To what extent should he be either? For Peter, assuming these roles without the chance to examine them critically has created enormous pressures—perhaps the same pressures modern women and men face when they determine to "have it all."

## The Reflective Practitioner

Although he does not describe himself as "hypersensitive," Mike shares with Peter a sometimes obsessive self-consciousness about teaching. But whereas Peter's ruminations sometimes lack a reflective dimension, Mike is usually able to distance himself—at least to some extent—from the anxieties he is feeling. One way he does this is through writing. Mike is one of the few TAs in last year's group who actually enjoyed keeping a teaching journal, and who has continued the practice of writing about his teaching on a semiregular basis.

In the essay quoted at the beginning of this chapter—the one in which he finds himself "staring blankly at the board, trying to figure out what the teacher was supposed to say," Mike undertakes to analyze in some depth those moments of fragmented consciousness that he sometimes feels as a teacher. The particular moment he writes about is one I remember from our conferences. At the time—about three weeks into the semester—he had described it this way:

> I had another one of those moments the other day when I was teaching. I hate talking. I hate, hate, hate lecturing, you know. But I was very straightforward, said, "I'm gonna bore you to death today, I'm gonna lecture. This is, we're doing memos and you

need to understand this stuff, I know I assigned the reading but everybody's got questions and some people won't ask them so— here it is." I tried to involve people in it, you know, ask questions back and forth and have some of them feed me the information, too. But mostly it was lecture. And I had a moment where I was up there talking, and I suddenly . . . fell out of that persona right in midsentence. And suddenly it just, sorta like almost an out-of-body thing where I just saw the class, and I saw myself, and I saw myself speaking and I stopped thinking of myself as a teacher . . . It was like I dropped out of it and just became super aware of myself as a lecturer, as somebody talking, as somebody imparting information, and there was also, part of it was somebody who didn't really know what they were talking about, even though I did. I knew exactly what I was talking about. But I suddenly had this fear that I didn't know what I was talking about, and I thought, "My God I'm just gonna freeze up here—I'm just gonna go blank and lose my train of thought and not be able to say anything and not know where I'm going."

When I read this transcript now, I am aware of the contrast between the nervous, disjointed pace of this oral account of Mike's experience and the slow, dream-like movement of the written version. Of course, the medium itself accounts for much of the difference. We are always dismayed, reading transcripts of our recorded conversations, to hear ourselves sounding like Richard Nixon on the Watergate tapes. But it isn't *just* the medium that makes the difference here, as Mike himself has observed. By the time he comes to write about his experience, he has taken a particular perspective on it, and that perspective leads him to see it as part of a pattern in his teaching, one of a series of similar moments when he confronts what he calls his "inadequacies as a teacher." These moments occur most often, Mike says, when he is lecturing— "which I hate to do"—and gets "tripped up" by a student question or a mistake of some kind.

For Mike, paradoxically, these painful moments in which he suddenly "sees himself" from a distance are connected to his inability to "see himself as a teacher." As he puts it:

> *I see these moments now as a kind of growing pain. As I am trying to find out who I am as a teacher, I am forced to do so from the position of student, since that is the closest thing to a teacher I have previously experienced. What this means, I think, is that I am only able to make brief forays into the teacher persona. I have a much closer identity with the students, and this sets up a conflict in the classroom between me-student and me-teacher.*

As I read Mike's essay, an analysis of "self" and "other" in this conflict, I am impressed with its level of psychological sophistication. In some ways, it deepens and extends Peter's metaphor of the TA sitting in the doorway of the faculty meeting. But again, as with Peter, I suspect that there may be other factors to consider here—factors having to do with how Mike conceives the role of the writing teacher.

### Teaching as a Political Act

Mike himself alludes to the role of the teacher when he writes about trying to *"create this persona in relation to society (or my perceptions of society) and its views (or perceived views) of teachers."* Since Mike didn't pursue this subject in his essay, I can't be sure, but it sounds as if his graduate reading in critical theory and cultural studies has sensitized him to the part that ideology plays in anything having to do with education.

That ideology *is* a factor in Mike's construction of the teacher persona cannot be denied. It permeates, in a subtle way, all our discussions of the difference between "Business and Technical Writing" and the first-year composition courses that he taught last year, but it emerges directly only late in the semester, when Mike has begun to think about plans for his second semester Composition II class. At that point, talking about a video he wants to show, a feminist critique of MTV, he says,

> Yeah. Yeah, I'm gonna show it in every class I teach. Very Elbowian philosophy. Teaching is political. My teaching is political. I'm not gonna lie to myself, I'm not gonna lie to my students. . . . I want them to know what my attitude toward the video is in the beginning. . . . That's the part of the education that, seems to me that that should be happening. It doesn't matter what class it's in, there should be something, you've always got dead time, I don't have every minute of every class planned and filled up with things that need to be taught so that people will learn everything they need to know about writing, you know, and I'd just as soon fill it with stuff that they need to know anyway.

The fact that Mike associates being "political" with Peter Elbow, a writer who has been criticized for not being political enough, might strike some as surprising. But there are reasons for that association that I will return to presently. In the meantime, the passage is interesting for a couple of other reasons. First, it makes clear that Mike's image of the teacher includes a healthy dose of social responsibility; he believes in giving students "stuff they need to know" to critique their culture. Second, it suggests that this "stuff they need to know" is separate from "everything they need to know about writing"—a distinction that implies an image of "writing teacher" that appears to be ideologically neutral.

This distinction may help explain why Mike has so much trouble assuming the teacher persona. If the "teacher" in Mike's mind is an enthusiastically political animal, the "writing teacher," in comparison, is a pale and bloodless creature. And it is "the writing teacher" whose persona he assumes in his "Business and Technical Writing" class.

Nowhere is the difference between these two roles more apparent than in a midsemester interview when Mike expresses vague discomfort about the "Business and Technical Writing" course. It is already the eighth week of class, but Mike feels that the class is still "pretty nebulous," the way it was in the beginning. Although he's not quite sure why this is so, Mike says,

> It could be something to do with the material. In fact I'm sure of that, boy if I was teaching—looks like I'm teaching 102 next semester, which I'm really happy about, and I'm getting all kinds of great ideas.

As he goes on to talk about his ideas for next semester's 102 course, in this interview and in the weeks that follow, I can hear a huge difference in his level of enthusiasm. Comp II is a course he is truly excited about, but "Business and Technical Writing"—well, that class just feels "flatter."

It hadn't always seemed flatter. Earlier in the semester Mike was excited about teaching "Business and Technical Writing." Because it is a 200-level course, taken by sophomores, juniors, and seniors as an alternative to 102, he thought the students might be more serious than first-year students. He also felt more confident going into this course than he had going into 101 last year. "I know a lot more about, or I feel I know a lot more about "Business and Technical Writing," he said.

The first few weeks of class were difficult, but by the sixth week, Mike was "beginning to enjoy" teaching 209. Although his students had not proven to be as serious as he had hoped—some took advantage of his being late once to leave without turning in papers—their writing was progressing nicely, and he found 209 assignments, where "everything's broken up into nice little sections," much easier to grade than 101 papers.

From these kinds of comments, as well as others I have quoted in previous chapters, I could see how Mike was conceiving this "Business and Technical Writing" class. Though the catalogue defines it broadly, as a writing course "designed for students interested in professional careers," Mike saw it in a fairly limited way, as an opportunity for students to learn the "rules and formats" that govern the writing they will do in their professions. At the time, as I suggested earlier, I was puzzled by Mike's attraction to this "rules and formats" approach. It is not one we stress in our program, and given Mike's reaction to what he felt was the overly "structured" approach to writing advocated by the 101 textbook, I would not have expected him to take such an approach himself.

So I'm not surprised, here in Week 8, that Mike's enthusiasm for teaching the "Business and Technical Writing" course has waned. But I *am* surprised, given what I know of Mike, that his dissatisfaction takes such "nebulous" form and that it leaves him feeling "on shaky ground," stripped of most of his earlier confidence:

> I don't know anything about "Tech and Business Writing," that's not me, that's not me, I'm not a "Tech and Business" writer. There's a difference, you know, I mean when I'm in, when I'm teaching 102, that's the kind of writer I am: I write that stuff, I think that stuff, I'm interested in it, and I think of myself as that kind of a writer. With "Tech and Business" it's something that I can do and that I understand, but I'm not a "Tech and Business" person, somehow, it's a way of—so maybe that's it, that, because it's 209 I feel like I'm more of an imposter than in 102 or 101.

What, I wonder, accounts for this sudden shift in attitude? Is it really as sudden as it appears? Later, Mike will say it's because the course was new to him and that he will probably feel insecure with every new course he teaches—and he may be right. But if that were the only explanation, I would have expected him to be gaining confidence as the semester progresses, not losing it. That is what happened last year in 101. Why isn't it happening here?

Actually, I can imagine several answers to this question. One thing I notice when I go back to the transcripts is that by midterm, Mike is starting to feel anxious about his own work as a graduate student. This semester, it has turned out that nothing is due until the end of the term, which has left him relatively free for the first half of the semester but is beginning to worry him now. Plus, he's starting to think about writing a thesis and applying for jobs in the spring. With all this work hanging over his head, he's feeling pressure, yet he's too "scattered" to do anything about it: "I just don't feel like a student this year," he says. "Am I burning out or something? What is this?"

The possibility that this anxiety about his student role could spill over and affect his teaching is something that has occurred to Mike, and it is no doubt a factor in his newly expressed doubts about 209. But there is something about his language in this Week 8 interview that suggests another problem, as well. Increasingly, Mike is feeling like an "imposter" in his 209 class, and he's not sure why. First he says "I don't know anything about 'Tech and Business Writing.'" But then he says, "It's something that I can do and that I understand but I'm not a Tech and Business person." What does it mean to be a "Tech and Business person"? And why does Mike now feel he's "not a 'Tech and Business' writer" when at the beginning of the course he was feeling good precisely because he *had* done this kind of writing?

## Suspended Moments

One way to answer this question is to look again at those "suspended moments" Mike wrote about in his essay, the moments in which he "falls out of the teacher persona" and worries that he'll freeze and go blank. What interests me as I read through our transcripts is how these moments, so frightening to a new teacher, contrast with another set of moments Mike doesn't bring up in the essay he writes later. One instance of this contrasting experience occurs just a week earlier than the one he chose to write about. On this occasion, Mike has been talking about how it feels to teach "Business and Technical Writing," where he finds himself alternating between "moments of panic and feeling like I'm completely in control." The control comes from feeling more settled, "settled in that I know what I'm doing," he says, and it manifests itself in sudden moments like these:

> Every once in a while I get these moments, I hear myself up there talking and I'll think to myself, "God, I know what I'm talking about! I have something to say here." This is, you know, I impress myself sometimes, and I just get these moments where I sit back and listen and go "Hey, OK, I can do this, you know, this is good."

When I ask Mike exactly what triggers these moments, he explains it this way:

> When I'm talking about it, instead of taking responsibility for the book and trying to teach them everything that's in the book, just pulling the parts out that make sense to me or don't make sense to me, then suddenly it's a blend, and there's a personal connection there, with the things that I know and feel about writing myself. And so suddenly I tap into that and I'm going, you know, from a natural thing.

Notice how closely this passage parallels the one quoted earlier. Both moments occur "suddenly" when Mike is "up there talking"; both involve a separation of consciousness, in which he either sees or hears himself; both occur at moments when he "knows what he's talking about" and is "making sense" of the material. And yet one is described as a moment of "terrible fear" while the other is clearly a moment of pride. What accounts for the difference?

Again, Mike's language may be the key here. For him, as I reported in the last chapter, teaching feels best when it is "natural," when it "makes sense to me," "has a personal connection," and draws on "things I know and feel about writing myself." In the first instance, he may have known what he was talking about, but as he acknowledges at the time, he hasn't known it long.

> I'm in the process of discovering this information half a step ahead of them. I'm appropriating the language in that book. I think that's in a sense . . . that's what teaching is, is being able to appropriate all these different languages. You know we talked about that academic community in the [teaching seminar], when we were talking about Rose [*Lives on the Boundary*] and everything? And it's being skilled not only in learning a language, being welcomed into academia and academic language, but for me this teaching thing, with the textbooks anyway, and certainly with different subject matter— Because I understand writing personally. If I have to do any of the writing that I need, that I have assigned in any of my classes, I am capable of doing [it]. But I am not versed in the language and the concepts and the way of thinking about it that these textbooks are, so I'm sort of appropriating that language, 'cause that's what I'm asking them to read, and then I'm trying to make that mesh with what I understand about writing, but it's not a perfect fit because I'm only, I'm only coming across it maybe three or four days ahead of them, you know? I'm staying ahead of the class, I haven't read the whole book yet, and so I'm reading it, and then I'm taking notes and then I'm organizing those notes into lecture notes that I'm giving them. But you know as I'm going along it's like a word, a key phrase, or a concept that I haven't thought of before, that is absolutely brand new, according to the book, that sort of makes me feel this distance suddenly between what I'm saying and what I understand or feel.

Mike's analysis here is interesting for several reasons. For one thing, it reveals how new writing teachers, just like their undergraduate students, "appropriate all these different languages" when they enter an academic community. Even as Mike describes this phenomenon, his use of the word "appropriated" demonstrates what he has appropriated from the teaching seminar. At the same time, Mike's language also reminds us how strong the presumption is, even in a writing class, that the teacher's role is to lecture, and what powerful pressure the rhetoric textbook may exert on new teachers of writing.

## The Teacher in the Text

Actually, I suspect that all these issues are tied in together. For the teacher in Mike's mind, it isn't enough to understand writing personally, one must be prepared to talk about it authoritatively in the language provided by the academic community. But since the new teacher is not yet a full-fledged member of that community, he or she must appropriate that language from the text.

Unfortunately, this act of appropriation doesn't come easily. Paradoxically, when Mike himself tries to do it, to appropriate the language of the 209 text, he stops thinking of himself as a teacher and sees himself instead "as a lecturer, as somebody talking, as somebody imparting information." This is exactly the way he felt through most of 101 last year, and why that whole experience was so frustrating for him.

In his first semester of teaching 101, Mike says, somehow "everything was contained [in] that textbook." In fact, it was "the implied philosophy of that textbook and the invisible authors of that textbook who were the real teachers in my mind who knew this stuff and I didn't." He goes on to say,

> The only thing I could do at that point was—you just don't feel that you can rely on yourself, so you have to rely on the book, even though you always said you'd never do that, you know. I hate teachers who just follow the book! "Why am I in class? I could do this at home!" So then I sort of disguised it. I'd read the book and try to put it into my own terms. I had lecture notes and everything . . . I guess I sorta saw myself as maybe a proofreader and an editor and maybe a little bit of a coach or . . . something but not really a teacher, 'cause I didn't think I could teach that stuff, I didn't know it, in the same way that the people who wrote the book knew it.

Although he's a little appalled at having fallen into this trap, Mike thinks he understands how it happened.

> I think that's how it's presented to us in classes. I mean, you're taking a class in anthropology, it's probably the only class you'll take in anthropology . . . and here's the book for the course on this, and this is all the knowledge there is . . . and when you're done with that class then you're done with that information and you know how to do whatever it is you took that course to do, theoretically. I mean that's the way I've always thought about it I guess, subconsciously. So when I looked at the textbook, especially since I didn't think I knew how to teach writing at all, it was like, "Well, this must be, everything must be in here, so if I give

> them this, then . . . they will know how to write and it's not my
> fault if it doesn't work." I was very removed from that whole
> process, I was an intermediary, I wasn't a teacher really.

Fortunately, though, something that happened toward the end of the
first semester released Mike from his dependence on the text. As he
was teaching a lesson on descriptive language—the lesson that I mentioned in an earlier chapter—"something just clicked" and he found
himself teaching from what made sense "personally," as opposed to
what made sense "logically." As he puts it:

> Some of the ideas I had about writing were just as applicable and
> were often just saying the same thing the book said but in a
> different way, and that began to make it a little more meaningful.
> I sort of understood what I was doing at that point instead of just
> assuming that by following the book it would make sense.

Buoyed by that experience at the end of 101, Mike began to gain
confidence in his own expertise. In 102 second semester, he was able
to get away from the text and to draw on his own resources to teach
what he knew about writing—an experience that accounts for the
eagerness with which he anticipates teaching 102 next semester.

In the meantime, though, in 209, Mike's relationship with the text is
more ambivalent. Although he thinks he is no longer intimidated by
the text ("Boy, I don't do that stuff anymore!") I am sometimes surprised at how easily he defers to its authority. In the section on writing
memos, for instance, Mike requires his students to follow the text's
"rules" for appropriate memo format because the form seems "logical"
and consistent with what he knows about information theory. But at
the same time, he admits that the structure is not something he himself
feels comfortable with, and when he considers using that format to
write up his own assignment sheets, he quickly abandons the idea.

Still, I suspect there *is* a difference between the way Mike used the
text in the first semester, and the way he regards it now. In 101, he
didn't even try to connect with the text, he simply deferred to it. Now
in 209, he does try to understand it, to make its language his own:

> Sometimes . . . I throw that stuff out. I can't teach something that
> I don't believe, you know. . . . But everything that I give them I
> mean, I understand, makes sense to me. I guess that's what I do as
> I'm reading the whole thing. I'm reading along and, you know, I'm
> studying it, before I'm thinking about teaching it I'm learning it,
> I'm trying to figure out what it is and put it together with things
> that I know. Oh yeah, that makes sense, that makes sense, that
> makes sense, come across something that doesn't make sense and
> I have to think about it, and I sorta go into this little teacher mode
> and say, "Well what would I do with this?" you know, "I can't

understand this," you know. Then I go back into reading it and
sort of try and assimilate it somehow.

To some extent, as Mike acknowledges, his ability to claim expertise, to move away from the sources of authority he has habitually
deferred to, is a function of experience and the confidence it confers.
But as I listen to Mike talk about his teaching, I again suspect that there
is more to it than that. As he attends to his teaching, Mike develops
specific strategies that give him access to his own expertise. In some
cases, as with the memos, these strategies involve applying what he
has learned from the experts—in this case, the text he is using and the
course in learning theory he once took. But his most successful teaching moments come about when he has made "personal connections."

> And suddenly I'll have an idea that makes tremendous sense. . . .
> And then I'm so excited by the idea and I'm so immersed in what
> that would be and what I could learn from it and what everybody
> could learn from it, that it's just a matter of presenting that. I'm
> not teaching any—I'm not thinking of myself, "OK, how do I teach
> this paper?"—it's like I got this great idea, look at this great idea.
> . . . And that's the best part of it, is coming across one of those
> ideas and it just flowing naturally from that; there's no other way
> to do it, I mean, here's this idea and the only way to get it across
> is to do it this way and then let people do things, run with it, you
> know, and do whatever they want, and just sort of sit back and
> guide and nudge or whatever along the way. And that, then I'm
> conscious of—God, this is what teaching is, this is what I want to
> be doing all the time!

In moments like these, it is easy to share Mike's excitement. But it is
also worth noting that even as he describes this transcendent experience—a moment in which he *knows* intuitively "what teaching is"—he
is simultaneously disavowing, yet again, the role of teacher: "I'm not
teaching any—" he starts to blurt out. Then even he notices the contradiction.

## Embracing Contraries

Earlier in this section, in the context of Mike's remarks about the
political nature of teaching, I noted that his allusion to Peter Elbow
might strike some as surprising. After all, Elbow has been criticized by
David Bartholomae and others for giving insufficient attention to the
political and ideological implications of what it means to teach writing. But there is another sense in which Elbow has given his attention
to political issues, and that is in the context of individual empower-

ment. In *Embracing Contraries* (1986), Elbow writes about the power dynamic of the classroom, the pressures created on both student and teacher by the complex and often contradictory roles we feel ourselves compelled to play. In Mike's case, Elbow has helped him understand that he cannot abandon his own political nature when he takes on the teacher persona. To foist his political beliefs on his students would be unethical. But to pretend that he is *not* a person with strong political beliefs would only force his ideology underground, where it might color his teaching in dangerous ways. Instead, he must acknowledge both these roles, embrace them, and be clear to both himself and his students about when and how he moves from one to the other.

In the same way, Mike seems to have learned that he must both inhabit and disavow the role of teacher. He may feel uncomfortable assuming the writing teacher's role, appropriating the writing text's language, but as a new teacher he needs a vocabulary to talk about what he knows, and there is simply no other way to develop it. Still, I find myself wanting to warn Mike: There may be other dangers in assuming too readily a role so encumbered with negative images— teacher as lecturer, teacher as imparter of information, teacher as enforcer of rules. If we step into that role unaware, we may lose what is best in our teaching. And unless we occasionally forget who's "supposed to be the teacher," we may miss the delights that come from learning along with our students.

### Closet Philosopher

I have already spoken in chapter 2 of Meredith's reluctance to see herself as an English teacher. And, indeed, much of her reluctance, it seems, is theoretical—or to use her term, philosophical. Because she feels herself at odds with much that she sees around her, including her colleagues, the 101 text, the curriculum, and the general "worldview" of the university, Meredith is beginning to think she may be in the wrong field entirely. As she puts it:

> I don't know, maybe I'm not a teacher of writing. I mean, I don't—
> when I hear other people teaching, like Lee Kilmer [another TA]
> teaches with the door open, and I told Deb, I said, "I listen to her
> teach and I think, 'My God, I don't teach like that' [laughs]." I
> hope that's not what I'm supposed to be doing because—I don't
> know.

What teaching "like that" entails, Meredith doesn't explain here, but other comments give a clue to what she is resisting. At one point, playing devil's advocate, I ask her how she would respond if a colleague in another field questioned the value of the personal writing that she assigns. Almost immediately she is on the defensive:

> I'm gonna try and teach some grammar, but that—I rebel against that too, it's like, "Why should we spend the whole time teaching grammar?" What really are we, that's what I don't know. So I don't know, I mean I don't know how I would answer that person. I'd say "OK, you tell me what a teacher of composition is. How do you know what it is if you're a biology teacher, how are you so sure that you know?" I mean what would he say, what would they say? That we're supposed to teach—what do they think we're supposed to teach?

Clearly, Meredith has an idea of what she's "supposed to teach." She's supposed to teach "grammar"—a term she uses broadly to include not only the usual conglomeration of prescriptive usage and sentence structure, but also matters of style and form. "Well I don't want to teach grammar," she says. "I don't want to be a grammar teacher." And besides, she asks, why should we have to teach it? Why haven't they learned that before?

It's ironic, of course, that Meredith should express her rebellion against teaching grammar in the same terms that others use to assign it to English teachers: "Why should we have to teach grammar, why haven't they learned that before?" From the way she talks about "grammar" here and elsewhere, though, it's clear that this is not the major issue for her. The major issue, rather, is a political one. It has to do "not with writing but with writing *about what*"—and with who has the power to decide what we in English teach.

This is not the first time Meredith has brought up these thorny political issues. In our second interview, she was already speculating about the purpose of 101:

> We say 102 is writing from sources, so what does that make 101? Shouldn't it—isn't it really the case that 102 is academic writing, and 101 is, that we're just sort of playing around until we have to make them do 102 because 102 is like a—there's all this politics involved that we're supposed to be teaching people how to write for other courses. . . . I mean, that's what I conceive that 102 is— OK so we're making them write this way because they have to know how to write in other classes. I want to say "to hell with other classes," I mean, what about us? Don't we have our own thing to do? I mean, is there anything that we have, are we just a pawn or something for everybody else? I mean, is writing just a utilitarian thing?

The notion that writing is "just a utilitarian thing," that it's a "tool for the rest of the university" that eventually "gets tied back up to the job thing" is what Meredith really rebels against. And since this seems to be "the way the whole university system is geared now anyway," it's no wonder that she doesn't really see herself as an English teacher but rather as a "closet priest" or a "closet philosopher"—one who is "just using this [teaching English] as a facade."

What Meredith calls her "priest problem" her "theological thing" may have various levels of meaning. On the one hand, she seems half serious about wanting to be a priest. A converted Catholic, she tells me at one point that she would be "off in a minute" if the church changed its views on women in the priesthood—though later she says she didn't really mean it. Elsewhere, the priest in Meredith seems to get blurred with the psychotherapist. Aware that her personal assignments might seem "weird" to outsiders, she find in the textbook at one point a "nice safe assignment" to use. It's a "standard textbook assignment," she says, "and nobody can say you're making them, you're being a psychoanalyst or a priest or anything [laughs]."

As for her "closet philosopher" role—well, that may have various meanings as well. One instance in which she seems to assume this role is when she talks about her resistance to teaching traditional argument, a mode she is quite familiar with by virtue of her academic training. Part of that resistance derives from the frustration she feels at trying to teach, in just one paper, "the science of argument"—something she sees as a "whole thing in itself." But there's more to it than that. After all, she says, "I don't want to teach logic. That's why I'm not in philosophy."

But perhaps Meredith's resistance to argument goes beyond impatience with formal logic. At one point, referring to a conversation we had last year, she says,

> If I'm saying that I'm apolitical that's really impossible, you can't be apolitical. You always have to have some kind of politics. So, if I care about something then I'm gonna want to make an argument for it. So I'm not totally unargumentative, I guess. But maybe there's something about just being that way for the sake of being that way or something that gets me—I don't know how to teach that without feeling like I'm encouraging this combative type mentality, or— Does that make sense?

Another time, defending her own "expressivist" viewpoint against hypothetical criticisms from those who advocate teaching "academic discourse," Meredith talks about feeling uneasy with the whole notion of persuasion:

> What I have the problem with is the manipulation end of it, that what I think people are talking about is writing to make a point or writing to prove that blahblahblah and so you should believe blahblahblah because—I mean that's what I hear coming from the other side.

What bothers her more, however, is another suspicion she has—the suspicion that "there's some underlying worldview underneath this [pro-argument] side." That, she says, is what disturbs her most about teaching argument: "And that's where I want to say, 'Where does the nature of the thing itself dictate that I take a certain worldview?'"

When I ask Meredith how she would describe that worldview as different from her own, she responds,

> Well, I think it's very—"male" is what I was gonna say. I mean, that was right on the tip of my tongue, but I didn't put that through the filter. But I mean this objective—I mean when you said proof I suddenly thought "Oh, you mean objective proof, what counts as proof." Beliefs and feelings and these things don't count as proof; what we want is reason, we want a structured argument, we want premise, premise, premise conclusion, like . . . in logic class, and that's a very, maybe not just male but that, that assumes certain things about the world, that knowledge is only gained, the only knowledge that counts is this cerebral type of knowledge. Does that make sense? I mean, I think that's what gets me mad about this argument, because I feel like there's something unsaid on the other, there's something at work under there that's being—

What—downplayed? Covered up? Although Meredith doesn't finish her sentence, I think I understand what she's getting at. Here, then, is another perception that alienates Meredith from seeing herself as an English teacher. Not only is she expected to teach academic discourse, but there is "something unsaid," "something at work" in the conventions of that discourse that is at odds with her own worldview. The fact that she sees this something as "very male" is significant, I think—as is the fact that this perception slips "through the filter" she normally has in place.

## Teaching as a Woman

What Meredith means when she talks about putting things through "the filter" is that she is often careful to screen what she says in public—or at least she has been in the past. Recently, she's found herself being more open, with her students, with me, with everyone. In one of our earliest interviews, she talks about what this feels like:

> I guess my fear now probably is of babbling—because I used to be
> so nervous that I would write everything down exactly and have
> it all planned out and be very formal and have it very set, but now
> that I've started to feel more comfortable, more relaxed, I'm capa-
> ble now of standing up and babbling [laughs].

The new openness Meredith is experiencing here seems to have come
about for a number of reasons. For one thing, she's no longer a rookie.
The mere fact that she has taught for a while now may be helping her
to relax. For another, she's finding the style of teaching in the English
department more to her liking than the purely lecture mode she's used
to. But the main reason Meredith is speaking her mind these days may
have more to do with her personal life—and with her growing awareness of the part gender plays in her teaching.

I have already quoted from an interview in which Meredith speaks
about writing as a child—the sense that she would "get in trouble"
with teachers if she wrote personal things for school, and her determi-
nation not to do to her students what was done to her by those teachers. Although she doesn't, in this instance, describe "what was done to
me" in terms of gender (perhaps the filter is in place), I sense that this
may be at least part of what is on her mind.

As it happens, the particular interview in which these remarks
occur has overlapped with the tail end of my interview with Keith.
When Meredith arrives, Keith has just raised the question of how
gender affects teaching, and since we are nearly finished, I ask
Meredith to come in and join us. This is how the conversation pro-
ceeds:

> *Libby:* We were just talking about whether men—you and I have
> talked about this, too—whether a man gets more, has more
> kind of automatic sense of control or authority in the classroom
> than a woman has and whether size makes a difference.
>
> *Meredith* [to Keith:] Aren't they more intimidated by you than by
> me?
>
> *Keith:* Yeah, well, see I was just saying I'd like to find ways to
> minimize that because I would like the respect I get to be based
> on something other than that.
>
> *Meredith:* Oh, you should use it to your own advantage.

A few moments later, Keith returns to this subject:

> *Keith:* That's interesting though, she says, "Use it to your advan-
> tage."
>
> *Meredith:* Well, yeah, because I have to work hard to get them to
> [inaudible] that you just have by virtue of walking into the
> classroom. I mean—

> *Keith:* But then, if I were your student, just imagining myself, there would be qualities that you have that I as a teacher don't have, I mean, your soft-spoken presence.
>
> *Meredith:* That's good?
>
> *Keith:* For me, it would be, it would be very—disarming.
>
> *Meredith:* It would throw you off guard?
>
> *Keith:* Well it would take a lot of the tension out of the class.

What is apparent here is that both Keith and Meredith see disadvantages in the way gender constructs their relationships with their students. I'll have more to say about Keith's view of this in a bit. For now, it's interesting just to look at the language they both use unconsciously here: "It's disarming," "It would throw you off guard?" For Meredith, who is always "on guard," the classroom can be a dangerous place—a place where students and teachers "intimidate" each other and where male teachers use gender and size "to their advantage." Given who she is, though, Meredith is unlikely to reap such advantages. And she scoffs at Keith's suggestion that a "soft-spoken presence" might have some advantages of its own.

When Keith leaves, Meredith and I don't pursue this topic directly, yet it comes up almost immediately in another context. When I ask Meredith what is going on in her classes, she offers an update on a story she had told me earlier. One of her students, a somewhat belligerent male who had challenged her when she gave him an F on a paper, has "suddenly become very diligent, actually wrote some good papers, and his whole attitude has changed." When I ask her if she takes credit for this, she replies:

> Well, I'm sort of in shock because I stood up—what I thought I was doing was standing up for myself, I didn't really think it had anything to do with, with making him work harder; I really didn't care at that point whether he worked harder or not, all I cared about was if he would just leave me alone and stop intimidating me, I mean . . . I didn't expect it to affect his work, I thought he would just do what he had to do to get by, so I'm kind of in shock. It's like standing up for yourself [has] unexpected benefits [laughs].

As she says this, her pleasure is evident and it reminds me of her sense of pride in telling me the VCR story. A connection between "standing up for myself" and succeeding as a teacher is something she would never have expected, but once it happens, it seems to open the way for further revelations. By the end of the semester, Meredith can say,

> It's like there's this private world in my head, and there's this world out there and they used to be totally disconnected. They

seem to be sort of coming together. And that applies to everything, other areas of my life. Well, you know that. Teaching gets into everything.

At this point, it sounds as if Meredith has found her voice as a teacher. And having found her own voice, she is more than ever committed to helping her students find theirs—especially her women students. Near the end of the semester, commenting on how she has changed as a teacher since she began, she comments:

> And that's another thing I've noticed that's very interesting this time, is that I seem to be concentrating more on women students, and I think the reason is being aware . . . that there had been this research done, that even female teachers would call on male students and use male students' names more than female students'. And that really bothered me. I thought, "Well do I do that?" I guess because I immediately felt guilty like I probably do do that. . . . And I would go back and forth, there would be some days when, I can remember a couple of days when I just made all the women talk [laughs], but then I realized that with the papers that female students seemed to be writing better papers this year, and that maybe I was doing something—this was in the afternoon class though—I mean you never know what causes what, but, but I wondered if maybe I was acting on that somehow, that I was getting these better [inaudible] from the female students. I went off on a different tangent, didn't I?

Now, with the perfect vision of hindsight, I can see where this tangent is leading Meredith. Within months she will decide to leave the graduate program in English, in search of a life, a career more compatible with her "worldview." Still, I don't think this move away from our program is a move backward for Meredith. In fact, I tend to see her new mentoring interest in her women students as a "tangent" only in the sense that all her most productive moves as a teacher have been "tangential"—that is, diverging from an original purpose or course. In her case, the "original course" might have been the traditional writing course, with its emphasis on grammar and form. Or it might have been the original course of her teaching career, in which the lecture was her predominant teaching mode. In each of these instances, to see herself as a teacher, Meredith first had to dissociate herself from one image—teacher as grammarian, teacher as lecturer, teacher as male—before she could construct another that felt compatible with her worldview. The fact that she eventually chose not to pursue this construction project probably says less about her as a teacher than it may about the rest of us. To what extent have we compromised our worldviews, I wonder, to see ourselves as teachers?

## More Conflicting Images

Although Meredith herself seems reluctant to define herself as teacher, Keith sees in her the teacher he would like to be. Or at least part of that teacher. Actually, Keith, like Peter, seems to hold in his mind several different images of the teacher, and these images are not always easy to reconcile.

The teacher that Keith admires in Meredith is the "soft-spoken presence" he comments on in the conversation quoted above. For him, this presence is definitely female, and in that respect it is harder to access than another image that he sees embodied—literally—in his favorite teacher from undergraduate school, Rosco Thorp. In the reflective essay he wrote for last year's teaching seminar, Keith described Thorp's powerful presence this way:

> *If any teacher ever commanded the respect of students because of physical presence alone, it was Rosco. He was a huge man. But the magnitude of his physical presence was not based only on sheer size and bulk. After all, many men are big. But Rosco was beyond big. Every inch of the man exuded strength and tenacity. And he quite simply looked mean. Rosco stood about 6'5" and weighed an even 300 pounds. His weight was surprising since he had lost a leg during World War II. But even with one leg, he was more of a man physically than most men who had two legs. Years of using crutches had thickened his furry arms to the size of a normal man's legs. His hands looked like huge calloused paws. Rosco's bald head stood out in contrast to his thick, jet-black beard, grizzled by a few rogue silver hairs. Dark eyes gleamed out of his craggy, scowling face. Taken as a whole, his demeanor was one that prompted most men to get out of his way. He was the only man I've ever seen who could walk through a densely crowded bar as if no one were there; a path would open for him as if miraculously. He moved through crowds like Moses moved through the Red Sea.*
>
> *Rosco's method on the first day consisted of lumbering slowly into the classroom on his crutches, sitting down on the desk at the front of the room and silently scanning the intimidated faces. After a few minutes he would sort of snort, and only then would he begin to call roll in his deep, resonant voice. Shortly into the class period he would begin to talk about American literature and would usually read a few of his favorite poems. His eyes would twinkle and a smile would replace his usual scowl as he dramatically boomed out Carl Sandburg or Emily Dickinson in his deep bass. Students were able to glimpse the soft heart under the tough exterior. But no one ever forgot that this was Rosco's class. He was the boss. Those who didn't like this arrangement were free to drop.*

Although he sees himself as no match for Rosco physically, Keith comes closer to fitting this image that most of us would. At 5'10" and 260 pounds, with the build of a veteran bodybuilder, Keith knows he has a commanding presence in the classroom. And, as Meredith suggests, he is willing to use it to his advantage when he has to. But he has also been aware, even from the beginning, that his physical presence can be a disadvantage. For one thing, it suggests a "tough guy" image that just doesn't suit his style. In the story he tells of his first day of teaching—the story from which the above passage is quoted—Keith reveals what happens when his attempt to imitate his hero, Rosco Thorp, falls through:

> *Everything was working. I looked tough. I sounded tough. And then I began to explain my philosophy of teaching, such as it was. As I talked about the workshop concept and the importance of revision, I began to look closely at my students' faces for the first time. In their faces I saw the faces of friends and people I knew. A few of the guys in the class reminded me of some of the high school students that I had coached in lifting over the years. They looked like such a nice bunch of people. I wanted so much to just sit and chat and get to know them, but what about being tough? The charade was becoming harder and harder to maintain. And then something slipped through the veil. "Don't think of me as a teacher," I said. "Think of me as a coach—a writing coach."*
>
> *That did it. Before I had any idea what I was doing, I undid everything I had worked so hard to accomplish with the big first impression. I continued rambling on, talking about how I cared deeply about the progress of each and every student, about how they could all feel free to call me at home at anytime, about how I hoped we could all get to know each other and have a good time in class during the semester. My God! I was being nice. I was being—myself.*

What is interesting about the story Keith tells here is how neatly it's all tied up. As the class goes on, one of the students addresses him as "coach" and he likes the sound.

> *Coach? No student would have ever called Rosco Thorp coach! I was shocked. I was disappointed. But then I realized that I liked the sound of that title—coach. And the students liked the sound of it too, as many of them quickly began using the title when addressing me.*
>
> *When I finally dismissed my class on that first day, I felt good. What seemed at first like a failure was really no failure at all. I had made the mistake of believing that I had to build some sort of classroom persona to hide behind and I had modeled this persona on Rosco Thorp, a person very much different from the real me. I discovered that I didn't have a classroom full of scheming, designing students who were out to usurp my authority and make me look like a fool. My students were real people with real problems, real feelings, and real fears. Most of them were probably as nervous about that first day of English 101 as I was. More importantly, I was reminded of something I should have been well aware of: I can't wear a hat that doesn't fit. In other words, if I can't be me in the classroom then I'm cheating both myself and my students. In spite of all my efforts to be someone I was not, I still managed to be myself. I still*

*managed to show my student the genuine Keith Williams on that first day. We went on to have a fun semester. We got to know each other very well. I even got some calls from students at odd hours of the night. I wouldn't have had it any other way. Most importantly, they became better writers and I became a better teacher, all because my real self was able to shine through.*

*Rosco Thorp was a vital influence on my life. He is also a good friend. Without his tutelage, I would probably have never considered a career in teaching. But I discovered on that first day that I can't walk forever in his shadow, always following in his footsteps. Rosco is Rosco and I am Me. And Me is all I ever have to be.*

Rereading Keith's essay a full year later, I note with interest the essentialist concept of self in this narrative—"the genuine Keith Williams," "my real self," "the real me." But by the time I become aware of that language, Keith himself has already moved away from it. He is also moving away from the image of teacher as coach that he had seized on back then. One way to see the change in his thinking is to look at his metaphor of the hat. In the narrative, the lesson is simple: "I can't wear a hat that doesn't fit." By the following fall, however, the matter of the hats has become a little more complex. Referring to a student in one of his classes, whom he has had to speak to rather sharply, Keith observes:

She just needed somebody to put their foot down once, which I did, and she respected that but I didn't like having to do it, I didn't think it was something I should have to do. I guess I realize if you're gonna be a teacher now and then you're gonna have to put on a different hat and be nasty, but I didn't like having to do it. I felt, "How dare you ask me to put this hat on?" But it was all right after that.

While before Keith seemed to be looking for an all-purpose hat to wear day and night, he's now acquiring a wardrobe of hats he can slip on and off as needed. The coach's hat is one of these, but it's clearly not appropriate for all occasions.

### The Coaching Model

It was in the beginning that the coaching hat was most appropriate for Keith. Then, he says "I knew nothing . . . and I wanted some sort of model or guide I could follow and that's the only one I had any experience with." The coaching model, which Keith sees as basically "a way of dealing with students" seemed perfect because the coach is somebody who, I mean, when I wrestled I still sometimes wonder what it was that kept me at it in the beginning, because I didn't like it, it was hard work, and the coach always keeps you motivated somehow to show up, practice, and put everything you've got into it while you're there. And sometimes I think that's all a writing teacher can do at times, if you assume that the best way to become a better writer is first of all to write.

In addition to the motivating factor, the coach has other strengths as well. When I ask if there are "techniques" that the coach taught him too, Keith responds,

Yeah. Yeah. And I always—and there is one person who I always, when I think of a coach I think of him. And the teaching was minimal. We'd be taught a very little, and then we would practice it over and over and over again. . . . I don't know to what extent I follow it. When I do show, teach a technique, it doesn't seem so much I'm teaching it but I'm showing it, as an example of what they can do, or what you, or "here's something you can try to liven up your writing a little bit." I had a teacher in [undergraduate school] who did that, and she used that Baker textbook, and looking at it now, it's a rather traditional textbook, but she would sort of, she would point out ways to make our, use more complex sentences, and it didn't seem like she was up there lecturing on grammar rules. It was like she was showing us something she wanted us to try, just to give it a try to see how we liked it. And I learned a lot from that, but I don't think I learned because she was teaching me but because she showed it to me in an interesting way and then I started practicing.

Interesting here is the distinction Keith draws between "teaching" and "showing." Like the distinction between showing and telling that we are all familiar with, this is clearly a distinction that privileges the showing. By implication, it reduces teaching to "lecturing on grammar rules"—something that should clearly be kept to a minimum:

For me, to be a coach is to be someone who gives a little bit of teaching but a lot of support. It's brief intense periods where you're teaching things, but the rest of the time you're pushing the student out onto the wrestling mat or the field or whatever to take what he or she has learned and put it into practice, and then correcting where necessary.

At the same time he finds the coaching metaphor attractive, though, Keith concedes that it has its limitations. For one thing, thinking of himself as "more of a friend, a coach, than a teacher" has made it difficult when the time comes to give low grades. And for another, the coaching model doesn't fit every class equally well. The "Business and Technical Writing" class he's teaching this semester "requires more teaching than Comp I," he says, by which he seems to mean that it requires "taking some material and presenting it to the class."

Another limitation of the coaching model is other people's reactions to it. Keith knows that not everyone has such a positive view of coaches as he does. Some of Keith's students—especially the women— seem to bristle when he uses sports metaphors, and one of his fellow male TAs "doesn't like it at all." Keith understands these reactions. "Some people might have a negative view of what a coach is," he says, "and others might feel excluded because they have no familiarity with coaches." The notion that he himself might have some of these same negative reactions is not one that occurs to Keith, though it does occur to me as I read our transcripts—and especially as I listen to him talk with Meredith.

My first sense that there is more communicated in the coaching metaphor than Keith himself is aware of occurs in one of our earlier conversations, the one in which Keith remarks on the difficulty of giving low grades while acting as "a friend, a coach." Encouraging him to pursue his analogy, I ask if there is anything coaches do that is equivalent to giving low grades, and he tells me about a time he got suspended from a wrestling tournament because he lost his temper when he allowed himself to be pinned by an opponent who was in better shape. When I suggest that this sounds more like a disciplinary measure than an actual grading situation, he agrees:

> Yeah, that's true. It seems like a coach more, the bad grades come out in verbal fashion. You just—I don't remember many coaches I've had or I've seen, who compliment as much as they criticize. You build up for a big event of some kind and all you hear is negative stuff about how badly you've been practicing, and how you better get your mind on what you're doing, and things that make you—but in a way that it's not so negative that you give up, you work harder. Then after the event you hear all these positive things, how "You worked really hard for this," and "I'm proud of you" and all that.

Although Keith apparently sees nothing negative in his characterization of the coach here, I sense a certain poignancy in his voice when he admits, "I don't remember many coaches I've had or I've seen, who compliment as much as they criticize." If this is indeed the case, then it's easy to see why not everyone would feel positive about the coaching model, and why Keith himself might feel some unacknowledged dissatisfaction with it.

It is not until the conversations with Meredith, however, that Keith begins to explore that dissatisfaction. Or perhaps this is the wrong language. For Keith doesn't so much express dissatisfaction with the coaching model as express interest in others. Just as he still dons the Rosco Thorp hat for those occasions when he needs to "put his foot down" with certain students, he's still fairly comfortable wearing the coach's hat. He just senses a need to add others to his wardrobe.

### Teaching as a Man

I've already mentioned the occasion on which Keith and Meredith began their conversation about gender roles and teaching. It was one of those happy accidents that generate food for thought on all sides. For Keith, though, these conversations seemed to hold special import. It was he who suggested that we all meet together and continue the conversation over the following two weeks. And it was he who would say, at the end of the semester:

> I enjoyed the interviews especially with Meredith because it was like point/counterpoint sometimes. We seemed to understand each other, but it's almost like a mutual admiration. We admire in each other the things we don't see in ourselves.

What Keith seems to see in Meredith, and in certain women teachers he has had, is a nurturing persona—not a mothering one, he is quick to say—but

> a teacher that, if you don't feel like participating, if you're intimidated by other students as I often was when I was a kid, you get a teacher who somehow, it's not exactly a mothering instinct, but just such a nice gentle way of drawing you out and making you feel secure at the same time. I could never do that.

In addition to having the "soft-spoken presence" he has mentioned earlier, such teachers are "quiet" and "nonthreatening." In their classrooms he could "feel comfortable" and "express myself without worry."

To Meredith, this characterization comes as a bit of a surprise. She is not sure she sees herself as a "nonthreatening" teacher, and though her goal is certainly to get the students to "express themselves without worry," she is often frustrated in her pursuit of that goal. Although she is clearly pleased that Keith sees her so positively, she suspects that he may not understand the disadvantages that go along with that soft-spoken presence. And perhaps he doesn't.

Though he begins by setting this whole discussion in the context of gender, Keith keeps slipping during the conversation into talking about personality. At one point, Meredith catches him up on that:

> *Libby:* Well Keith, you suggested this mutual meeting so what have you been thinking about?
>
> *Keith:* I have just been thinking about how your perspective [to Meredith], I mean you said that I should take advantage of the fact that— [*Meredith:* "Oh, yeah."] I would think I interpret what you're saying, that you think I can probably intimidate a lot of students.
>
> *Meredith:* Well you have an advantage going in because they will automatically pay attention to you, you don't have to prove, there's something that you don't have to prove that I have to spend a lot of time proving, it seems to me, before I can get to the next point, or something like that. Does that make sense?
>
> *Keith:* Well, see, I think that you see advantages in my personality, I see advantages in yours, and I don't think either of us appreciate totally the [*Meredith:* "I'm not talking about personality."], I mean what we see as weakness . . .
>
> *Meredith:* I'm just talking about your physical size and the fact that you're male.

A bit later, Keith makes clear why he doesn't see this as entirely a gender issue:

> Well, some—there are some teachers I've had, female teachers who seem to me like they're probably quiet people but maybe were trying to assert themselves so much that they came across as threatening, in a way.

In Keith's view, it is not gender but personality that is at issue. Even women teachers can be so assertive that they intimidate students. And men—well, men can be soft-spoken presences, too, can't they?

In fact, Keith's experience suggests that he may have less control over the image he projects than he thinks. At one point, talking about the way he's perceived by others, he acknowledges this himself:

> *Keith:* A few weeks ago a friend of mine who is really knowledgeable about psychology and all that stuff described me as assertive [laughs]. I thought I was totally the opposite of assertive, because I don't like assertive people. Assertive means pushy.
>
> *Meredith:* Well that's, yeah, that is assertive.
>
> *Keith:* So I have perceptions of myself, I don't see myself as others see me.

Still, Keith is reluctant to see the larger implications of what he's saying here. The notion that he still sees differences in terms of personality rather than gender is evident in a comment he makes at the end of the semester. Looking back on the interviews with Meredith which he has found so productive, he says:

> Boy, she and I seem to be on opposite sides of the fence as far as
> our, our approach. I mean, because of our personalities.

But he's intrigued by the whole issue, and as he struggles awkwardly
to explain it to me at the end of the semester, it's apparent that he's at
least willing to consider that it might be more complex than he's so far
acknowledged:

> One interesting thing that I'd like to talk to Meredith more
> about—maybe we could do something with the writing aspect—is
> there are several times we talked about the role gender plays in
> the classroom as far as your persona and power in the classroom,
> and I wonder if that's—'cause she really sees it as something that's
> a real problem and I, I've always seen it as something— When
> she's trying to, she would like to be in my position, to—I don't
> know, not necessarily to be male—the advantages of being, of my
> presence as opposed to hers, whereas I see advantages to her
> presence. And I wonder if there are some inescapable things in-
> volved with gender and teaching, or if there are ways to, if it's, the
> problems are in ourselves or if they're actually deep-rooted in
> society to such an extent that in the classroom there is this real
> structure that at this point there's not much you can do about. To
> what, I'm sure it's in the classroom, but to what extent is it [tape
> runs out and he continues to talk as it's turned over] or the extent
> to which we feel it a problem ourselves, as a teacher, which, which
> is the one we have to work out first. I would think how we see it
> in ourselves—but on the other hand, maybe even if somehow we
> came to terms with it in such a way that we were comfortable with
> it, it still isn't gonna work in the classroom—who knows?

Although Keith's thinking isn't easy to untangle here, its tangled nature suggests the complexity of the issue he is considering. Is gender,
in fact, "inescapable"? Are the problems it sometimes raises in the
classroom "in ourselves," or are they "actually deep-rooted in society"?

At this point, Keith is inclined to believe the problems *are* in ourselves, or rather, in our perceptions. As he says a moment later:

> So maybe it is just a situation where it's what we perceive or think
> we perceive, or what we feel inside as a teacher. 'Cause you're
> never gonna make every student comfortable in the classroom,
> but the teacher of all people should be comfortable if anyone is.
> 'Cause I sometimes wonder if some of these concerns make it
> difficult for Meredith to perform in the classroom the way she
> wants to, and to do the kind of job she has in mind of doing in the
> classroom. I wonder if these really do get in the way of this, to any
> great extent.

As I listen to Keith speak, I wonder to what extent his perceptions are shaped by his own gendered experience. As a gay male, he is certainly sensitive to the "deep-rooted" attitudes about gender that shape our relationships both in and out of the classroom. When he resists Meredith's tendency to see the role of teacher as "inescapably" shaped by gender, is it perhaps just Meredith's two-gender construct that he resists? When Keith himself encounters this question, reading an early draft of the manuscript I am preparing, he is intrigued by its implications. Over the past few months, he has noticed that his "thinking about being a teacher" has developed in interesting ways. More and more he finds himself thinking about "how much of myself is hidden from my students, and what a fine line I walk."

## Conclusion

As I watch these TAs go through the process of becoming teachers, negotiating their identities among what Deborah Britzman (1991) has called "a cacophany of past practices, lived experiences, cultural myths, and normative discourses" (59), I reflect on the question I began with. What is it we share, those of us who are reluctant to see ourselves as teachers? With these TAs, I realize, it's more than lack of confidence—it's also ambivalence. They're not sure they want to be teachers, given the way our culture sometimes defines that role. Teachers are lecturers, disciplinarians, grammarians, authority figures. They would rather be friends, foster parents, coaches, priests, or therapists—all roles that they see more positively than the teacher role, all roles that they can see themselves performing in some way.

I can understand their ambivalence. In my own case, reluctance to see myself as a teacher seems tied to a similar dissatisfaction with the role of teacher as disseminator of information. For years I have attributed this ambivalence to a personal failure. Somehow, I could never retain information long enough to pass it on to my students. Whenever I found myself in the lecturer mode, presenting background information on the English Romantic movement or distinguishing between expressivist and epistemic approaches to teaching writing, I would close the classroom door, afraid some colleague would walk by and hear what a fraud I was. But listening to my TAs talk about their teaching has given me another way of thinking about this ambivalence. Maybe it wasn't my colleague in the hall whose judgment I feared, but my own. Maybe I did know enough to be a teacher—I just didn't know what I knew.

Now, having acknowledged my ambivalence, I am better able to deal with it. I can imagine new teaching roles for myself—roles that are more consistent both with who I am and with what I believe about teaching. Some would say, perhaps, that my ability to take this perspective is a function of age and experience—that I have time now to reflect, and a wide range of teaching experience to reflect upon. But that's not the whole story. For the fact is, I have learned an enormous amount simply by talking with these young TAs. Listening to them, I have learned to listen to the voices within me. Watching them grow into their roles, I have learned to see myself as a teacher.

# Interchapter:
## Seeing Myself as a Researcher

When I began this project, I wasn't sure what I was doing. At one point, writing a grant application and casting about for a way of describing the "specific objectives" of my research, I wrote:

*This study seeks to describe and analyze the experiences of five graduate teaching assistants in a college composition program. Its purpose is to gain insight into the ways these teachers construct their knowledge of their discipline, develop their teaching skills, and negotiate the formation of their professional identities.*

There is something awful about the sound of that paragraph. In a sense this *has* been the object of my study, and yet these aren't the purposes I began with. These are purposes I constructed later, to satisfy those who give research grants and put together conference programs. My project began in another place entirely, reading with fascination these TAs' journals, wanting to sit back and read and listen more.

As the project evolved, I did develop general questions: What is it like to teach writing as a new TA? What is on new teachers' minds? How do they integrate who they are with what they do as teachers? How can we make it easier for them? How can we help them become their best teaching selves? And all the time, in the background, another set of questions: What can I learn about myself from listening to these new teachers? What can all of us learn about ourselves?

———————

One late afternoon in January, I am at Florida State University, sitting in on Wendy Bishop's graduate research seminar. This is another of my leave projects: visiting writing programs at other campuses around the country, looking for ideas we can use in our program.

The graduate students are engaged in a collaborative study of first-year creative writing classes and are reporting on ethnographic research in progress. After one report, someone observes that the students in creative writing classes seem to identify as writers more readily than do students in regular composition classes. They talk about why this might be so, and I offer an observation from my interview project. It surprised me, I say, that the TAs I talked with seem so reluctant to think of themselves as teachers. At first I thought it was just lack of confidence; then I realized that it's also ambivalence: they're not sure they *want* to be teachers, given the way our culture sometimes defines that role.

And then suddenly I am saying something more: It's like me with research, I tell them. It's a word I almost never use. Though I am clearly engaged in two research projects, I don't think of myself as researcher. And though part of that may be due to lack of confidence—a lack I can't really attribute to being new to the role—I think another part may be due to a similar ambivalence—an ambivalence about what it means to be a researcher in our academic culture.

As I think about what I've said later—what I've confessed to this roomful of strangers—I find that I've stumbled onto something. I do resist the role of researcher, and I'm not sure why. But it does seem connected somehow to the image of researcher I carry around in my head. What is that image I carry, and where does it come from?

---

When my sabbatical leave officially began last summer, one of the first ritual tasks I undertook was to clear out my office in the English department and move to a private study—a narrow, windowless office on the fourth floor of our university library. That a researcher was one who "holed up" in libraries was an unquestioned assumption for me, though once I got there, I didn't quite know what to do. Clearly, there was plenty to read on the subjects I was interested in—ethnographic research, pedagogical theory, case studies of new teachers at all levels of education—and yet I wasn't really excited about doing this reading. After a few desultory swings through the on-line catalogue and the CCCC bibliography, dutifully noting relevant citations on the little slips of paper provided at the computer stations, I found myself spending less and less time in the library. The texts I most wanted to read were not there.

As the year went on, I did find myself going back to the library from time to time, following up on a colleague's casual reference, tracking down a book I had seen advertised. But my reading seemed far too unsystematic to qualify as "research." I have long pages of notes on Donald Schon, for instance, but far fewer on Wendy Bishop and Deborah Britzman, whose case studies of teachers may have influenced me more. I have no notes at all on Peter Elbow's *What Is English* (1990), which inspired the notion of "interchapters" in this book, nor on Lad Tobin's *Writing Relationships* (1993), which I read in manuscript and which not only confirmed my ideas but helped me find my voice. Even as I write the section you are reading, I am aware of all I *might* have read for this project but didn't: the feminist theory a colleague saw as essential to certain sections, the research on teacher socialization I learned about serendipitously from a colleague in another field. And yet . . .

And yet if I had it to do all over again, I doubt that I would do it very differently. Sometimes, we just have to make our own choices, construct our own professional identities as we go along. It's true that I've had to squint a bit to see myself as researcher . . . but little by little, the image is becoming clearer.

# Afterword

## Fall, Again

The new TA group gathers as usual for the 3 p.m. Monday practicum. Six women and four men this time, their ages scattered evenly along a continuum from twenty-two to forty-five. Despite the different ages, though—not to mention different temperaments and backgrounds—this group seems to have "clicked" from the beginning. Even now, as a lively discussion of portfolio grading grows louder and more combative, they interact like a big exuberant family around the dinner table—a far cry from the "dysfunctional family" my five interviewees came in with.

More than once this semester I have thought: If they had all been like this, I would never have started this project. And that's true. The dissonance I felt in last year's TA group prompted this project—but what I've learned in the process isn't just about those TAs. It's about all new teachers, maybe about teaching in general.

---

In the beginning, I would recite the ethnographers' mantra: "Trust your data," I would tell myself. "The meanings will emerge." Of course, I knew the meanings weren't simply lurking there, waiting to be discovered. They "emerged" as themes of my research only because I wrestled them forth, constructing and reconstructing them continually as I talked with the TAs, listening to our tape-recorded conversations, reading and rereading our transcripts.

When the theme of "taking it personally" emerged, I tried to hold it back. It wasn't, I thought at the time, really central to my purpose; it had little to do with teaching writing *per se*. And yet it kept coming back, in all our conversations, threading in and out of other topics, demanding my attention: taking it personally, caring too much for students, being angry and frustrated, feeling excitement and pride.

Finally, I turned and faced it: What the TAs were telling me was that teaching writing is a personal act. It engages the emotions, not just the intellect, and involves human interactions that cannot be separated from the other acts we perform as teachers of writing: constructing syllabi, planning classes, reading texts and responding to papers. In one sense, of course, this is obvious—which may be why I ignored it so long. But the fact is, we rarely talk about the personal aspects of teaching. Or if we do, we tend to talk behind closed doors, unloading our frustrations on colleagues, exulting over triumphs with friends and partners, admitting our fears and insecurities in private journals.

To some extent, these habits may be changing. As the field we call "English" broadens to include areas of inquiry like feminist theory and cultural studies, writers in academic journals and speakers at professional conferences are deconstructing the personal/professional dichotomy, and using teaching as the site of their explorations. I think particularly of essays I have read recently, by Nancy Miller and Jane Tompkins in literary theory, Lad Tobin and Nancy Sommers in composition. Though quite different from each other, these writers share a common agenda: exposing the hidden connections between who we are as people and how and what we profess to teach. Such an agenda, of course, has prompted reactions from critics who see it as "self-indulgent," "theoretically naïve," even "dangerous." And indeed it can be dangerous to talk openly about personal issues in teaching—or if not dangerous, then certainly awkward and difficult. But so be it. If our first attempts seem awkward, as they sometimes are, we must grow more sophisticated. We must find ways to read our own teaching, our relationships with students and peers, as carefully and as subtly as we read the other texts we are used to studying.

---

If I resisted the theme of "taking it personally" in the transcripts, the TAs themselves resisted theory, or so it seemed from our initial conversations. In their journals last spring, I had caught a brief glimpse of issues that interested them: the relative value of personal, creative, and academic writing; the virtues of freedom vs. structure in the classroom; the complex nature of pedagogical power and authority. I knew these ideas were still important to the TAs—I could sense their presence in the background of our conversations. Yet when we talked, they rarely raised such subjects on their own, and even when I brought them up, they seemed reluctant to pursue them. At first I didn't understand the nature of this resistance. But then it occurred to me that I may have helped create it. In the seminar we had called "theory" only those ideas expounded in our readings. The ideas the TAs held, the assumptions and values they brought to their teaching, were always secondary, always *responses* to theory, not theoretical in their own right. It was only natural then, that the TAs would think of theory as something alien to them, something to study in graduate courses, something, in many cases, to resist.

This year, as I returned to my work with the new TAs, I determined to change the way we talked about theory. Before the TAs even arrived on campus, I sent out letters, asked them to think about "What it means to teach writing." Although the questions I gave them didn't use the word "theory," they did raise theoretical issues: What are we doing when we teach "writing" in college? Where does writing ability come from? Is teaching writing the same as teaching literature? Psychology? Calculus? What does the writing teacher need to know and understand? What should be going on in a writing classroom? What should students be doing? What role should teachers play? What does it mean to "grade papers"? What kinds of teacher responses to writing are most helpful to students? What can we learn by thinking about our own school experiences? About teaching and learning apart from the context of school?

When the TAs arrived on campus, they were primed for discussion—discussions into which I would occasionally interject the term "theory" or "theoretical thinking." In the fall practicum, for example, when two TAs argued about the value of a teaching practice, I would often let them go for a while, then stop them and pose a question: What theories underlie the positions you're taking here? At what points are these theories in conflict? After class, the TAs wrote responses to our discussions, reflected in greater tranquility on the ideas they heard their peers expounding. At the end of the semester, I asked them to compile teaching portfolios, and to demonstrate in those portfolios their capacity for "theoretical thinking."

Did my new approach make a difference for these TAs? Did it decrease their resistance to reading and hearing about Theory with a capital T? I don't know. There are too many variables. Still, I like the kinds of thinking I heard in our discussions, and I like the way the TAs felt free to "go public" with their ideas. In their offices they would gather and argue vehemently with each other; in their classrooms they would explain their teaching philosophies to their students; in their teaching portfolios they would reflect on the philosophies that underlay their teaching practices. For the most part, the TAs still refrained from using the word "theoretical" to describe their own thinking. Like me, they seemed much more comfortable with terms like "philosophy of teaching." Still, I think they were doing the kind of thinking I had hoped for, seeing how teaching *is* based on theory, and how theory too derives from experience and is always in flux. In the end, perhaps it doesn't matter whether my prompting empowered the TAs' thinking—or whether it just empowered me to hear the thinking they had been doing all along. If, as Sara Lightfoot says, "Good teachers regard themselves as thinkers, existing in a world of ideas," then I believe these new TAs are well on their way to becoming good teachers.

---

What surprised me more than the TAs' resistance to theory was their resistance to the role of the teacher. Despite my own struggles to see myself as a teacher, I had never understood the extent to which that role frustrates and confounds us. My own struggles, I had always assumed, were due to personal inadequacy, a problem deep within *me*. Through the TAs, I began to see my resistance differently, to understand it as part of a larger phenomenon, part of the culture of teaching.

Recently, at the urging of a colleague, I wrote an article for a campus newsletter on this subject of seeing yourself as a teacher. In the article I talked about the imposter syndrome, and the difficulty some of us have negotiating our identities as teachers. Although I suspected that others would identify with what I was saying, I was still surprised at the number of responses I got. One note came from a colleague new to our campus: "Thanks for sharing your insights on teaching," she wrote. "I was just getting over feeling like an impostor at my last school. Now here I am, making it up as I go again. The scary thing is how believable my colleagues find me." A little later, at our office Christmas party, a male professor of religious studies with a quiet, self-assured manner confided: "You're right. Male teachers feel like impostors, too. I do, every time I walk into the classroom." In one sense, I find myself comforted by these admissions, pleased to have my ideas and reflections validated by others. But how sad it is that even committed veteran teachers can't fully inhabit their roles!

What would happen, I wonder, if we all came out of the closet, if we admitted our frustrations with the roles we play as writing teachers and threw our energies into imagining more attractive alternatives?

Would we find, as some of these new teachers did, generative metaphors to sustain us? I admit I cannot quite imagine myself as a coach or a priest or a stepparent. But there may be potential in another role I've been practicing of late. What ethnography requires of the researcher, it teaches the teacher as well: to suspend judgment, interpret generously, allow meaning to emerge. More than anything, though, it teaches us to sit back and listen—to hear ourselves in others, and to hear the Others within us.

# Works Cited

Britzman, Deborah. 1991. *Practice Makes Perfect: A Critical Study of Learning to Teach.* Albany: State University of New York Press.

Connors, Robert J. 1986. "Textbooks and the Evolution of the Discipline." *College Composition and Communication* 37.2 (May): 178–94.

Elbow, Peter. 1986. *Embracing Contraries: Explorations in Learning and Teaching.* New York: Oxford University Press.

———(1990). *What Is English?* New York: Modern Language Association of America; Urbana, National Council of Teachers of English.

Gere, Anne Ruggles. 1987. *Writing Groups: History, Theory, Implications.* Carbondale: Southern Illinois University Press.

Knoblauch, C. H., and Lil Brannon. 1984. *Rhetorical Traditions and the Teaching of Writing.* Upper Montclair, NJ: Boynton/Cook.

Rose, Mike. 1989. *Lives on the Boundary: A Moving Account of the Struggles and Achievements of America's Educational Underclass.* New York: Penguin.

Tobin, Lad. 1993. *Writing Relationships: What Really Happens in the Composition Class.* Portsmouth, NH: Boynton/Cook-Heinemann.

Tompkins, Jane. 1990. "Pedagogy of the Distressed." *College English* 52.6 (October): 653–60.

# Index

# Author

**Elizabeth Rankin** is associate professor of English at the University of North Dakota, where she is active in all phases of the university writing program.